THE BEST
Estes Park
HIKES

THE SHINING MOUNTAINS GROUP
of
THE COLORADO MOUNTAIN CLUB
with
WARD LUTHI

The Colorado Mountain Club Press
Golden, Colorado

The Best Estes Park Hikes
© 2013 by The Colorado Mountain Club

PUBLISHED BY

The Colorado Mountain Club Press
710 Tenth Street, Suite 200, Golden, Colorado 80401
303-996-2743   e-mail: cmcpress@cmc.org

Founded in 1912, The Colorado Mountain Club is the largest outdoor recreation, education, and conservation organization in the Rocky Mountains. Look for our books at your local bookstore or outdoor retailer or online at www.cmc.org/store.

Erika K. Arroyo: design, composition, and production
Eduard B. Avis: copy editor
Ward Luthi: project manager
John Gascoyne: series editor
Christian Green: publisher

CONTACTING THE PUBLISHER
We would appreciate it if readers would alert us to any errors or outdated information by contacting us at the address above.

DISTRIBUTED TO THE BOOK TRADE BY
The Mountaineers Books, 1001 SW Klickitat Way, Suite 201, Seattle, WA 98134, 800-553-4453, www.mountaineersbooks.org

TOPOGRAPHIC MAPS are copyright 2009 and were created using National Geographic TOPO! Outdoor Recreation software (www.natgeomaps.com; 800-962-1643).

COVER PHOTO: Lily Lake, near the trailhead, looking northwest. Photo by Dave Cooper

We gratefully acknowledge the financial support of the people of Colorado through the Scientific and Cultural Facilities District of greater Denver for our publishing activities.

WARNING: Although there has been an effort to make the trail descriptions in this book as accurate as possible, some discrepancies may exist between the text and the trails in the field. Hiking in mountainous areas—and canyons and deserts as well—is a high-risk activity. This guidebook is not a substitute for your experience and common sense. The users of this guidebook assume full responsibility for their own safety. Weather, terrain conditions, and individual abilities must be considered before undertaking any of the hikes in this guide.

First Edition

ISBN 978-1-937052-04-1

Printed in Korea

Two years—2012 and 2013—have great significance in the history of the Colorado Mountain Club. In 2012, the organization celebrated its first 100 years of existence and extraordinary achievement. In 2013, CMC began its next century of being the champion in the effort to preserve the best that Colorado has to offer.

The Colorado Mountain Club does, and stands for, many things:

Education—how to climb a rock face, how to navigate your way through the dark timber, and how to attend to backwoods medical needs.

Environmental stewardship—learning to walk softly across the land, and why and how Colorado must be preserved for future generations.

Innovation—CMC is a dynamic organization and adapts to present-day realities and changes while continuing to honor its fundamental traditions and mission.

It is with total regard that this pack guide is dedicated to The Colorado Mountain Club—its members, its objectives, and its mission. This pack guide also spans those two meaningful years—2012 and 2013. *The Best Estes Park Hikes*, a project of the Colorado Mountain Club Press, was kicked off in the summer of 2012. On June 21st of that year, enthusiastic members of the Shining Mountains Group of CMC met with Project Manager Ward Luthi, CMC Publisher Christian Green, and Series Editor John Gascoyne at the Estes Park Fire Department.

At that first meeting, much of the discussion focused on determining the 20 *"Best Hikes"* in, around, near, and/or reasonably reachable from Estes Park. After a good deal of discussion—and some serious negotiation—the top 20 hikes were chosen.

The columbine—our state flower.

Natural camouflage.

The next order of business was to select volunteers to hike these 20 trails. Most of the trails were adopted by those in attendance; ownership of a few more would come later.

By the end of 2012, all of the trails had been hiked, all of the photos had been shot, and all of the maps had been mapped out. The next task was to turn this trove of information into a useful and attractive hiking guide.

By the summer of 2013, the pack guide was available at many retail outlets and through CMC online at www.cmc.org/store

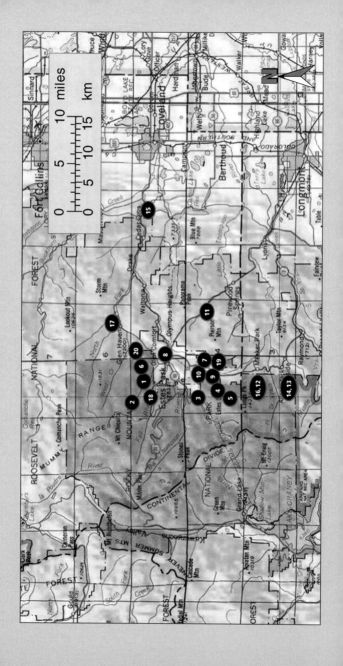

CONTENTS

A younger bobcat.

FOREWORD

In the winter of 2007, six seemingly long years ago, the Colorado Mountain Club Press embarked on an ambitious project. There was a perceived need to create highly portable, highly accurate, and attractive guidebooks for many hiking locales and destinations in Colorado.

These books, known as pack guides, would be the work product of various CMC groups throughout the state. Intended users, however, would include the general recreating public as well as our members.

The first such pack guide, *The Best Fort Collins Hikes,* was to serve as the prototype for the series. Working closely with members of the Fort Collins group, I had the privilege of being that book's editor.

Since that time, about 10 such pack guides have been published by CMC Press and I've served as series editor on these. The press has published a number of larger-sized hiking guides as well. Other pack guides, produced by veterans of the first books, are also being compiled.

Rocky Mountain National Park, very understandably, was one of the areas for which we wanted to produce a pack guide. After a good deal of discussion and deliberation, however, it became evident that Estes Park, a natural gem in its own right, warranted a separate pack guide—the book that you are holding.

The Best Estes Park Hikes contains hiking opportunities for a wide variety of enthusiasts—from the young and the neophyte to seasoned veterans looking for a bit of a challenge. As you scan this book, let your imagination run free and see which of these trails you want to do first.

Although they are mentioned elsewhere, the Shining Mountains Group of CMC, with a few special friends and under

Am I cute or what?

PHOTO BY MARLENE BORNEMAN

the direction of Project Manager Ward Luthi, deserve special recognition here. They were the people who, cameras in hand, hiked the trails, shot the photos, and produced the maps that appear in this book and in *The Best Rocky Mountain National Park Hikes*.

Special thanks are due to some folks who contributed photos to this book: Carol Glasson, Jon Quebbeman, and Dave Cooper, who took the cover photo. A number of photographs were contributed by Marlene Borneman, co-author of the CMC Press book *Rocky Mountain Wildflowers*.

To borrow a line from Roy and Dale: "Happy trails to you . . ."

—John Gascoyne
Series Editor

ACKNOWLEDGMENTS

Every single wild place in America is a treasure and, as a people, we're blessed to have a wealth of these wild retreats. In such places we can explore, have adventures, and come to know the wild creatures with whom we share this planet. Perhaps as important as anything else, these are places where we can rest, rejuvenate, and luxuriate in wild, untrammeled scenes of great beauty and inspiration.

Protecting our wild places has always been a noble and challenging venture. Special tribute and admiration must go to Enos Mills, the man often called "The Father of Rocky Mountain National Park." Enos made his first successful ascent of Longs Peak in 1885 at the age of 15, went on to homestead in the Estes Park area, and led the effort that resulted in the creation of Rocky Mountain National Park in 1915. The beautiful and tranquil Mills Lake, out of the Glacier Gorge trailhead in RMNP, was named in tribute to Mr. Mills.

Special tribute and admiration must also go to those passionate individuals and groups who have followed in the footsteps of Enos Mills. The dedication of these groups and individuals to wild places has helped preserve and interpret the magic of Rocky Mountain National Park for all who visit.

The Shining Mountains Group of the Colorado Mountain Club deserves high praise for their organized efforts to protect and preserve RMNP, instruct its members on minimum impact travel in wild areas, and teach basic wilderness skills to help members safely and enjoyably travel in the great outdoors.

Most of all, I would like to offer heartfelt admiration and thanks to a special group of individuals who have donated their time and effort and brought great passion to penning trail descriptions for our Estes Park pack guide. Smoky days from the many fires burning in Colorado this summer made hiking and photography a challenge at times. Through it all, they graciously accepted my questions and requests for further editing, and produced a book I hope will be enjoyed by many in the coming years.

Alan Apt	Renee Quebbeman
Amy Crow	Caroline Blackwell Schmiedt
Danielle Poole	Rudy Schmiedt
Nathaniel Potson	Sallie Varner
Jack Powers	Kurt Worrell

Another individual who must be singled out for his tireless work behind the scenes is my friend and editor, John Gascoyne. John graciously asked me to serve as project manager for this pack guide, not realizing, I suspect, how many times he would have to answer questions and provide guidance during the weeks and months we worked to put this guide together. John is a brilliant editor, tireless crusader for all things wild and free, and persistent in his effort to produce the highest and best in pack guides.

And to Christian Green, our publisher, a very large measure of thanks and gratitude for allowing me to be a part of a great tradition that is the Colorado Mountain Club.

I look forward to seeing all of you on the trails.

—Ward Luthi
Project Manager

Beauty on a branch.
PHOTO BY MARLENE BORNEMAN

Introduction

Hiking is my first love. But compiling descriptions of some of the world's finest trails is a close second. For me, putting this guidebook together was a labor of love—truly. But then, for me, exploring the great outdoors is what life is all about. I believe we do best when sitting around a campfire at night with family and friends—after exploring the great outdoors by day. Maybe you can remember your own nights in the woods, quietly staring into the glowing embers of a campfire, teasing your friends or family about who can make the best toasted marshmallow, all the while listening to the wind blow through the pines. If you haven't done this, I highly recommend you make it a priority in your bucket list of life goals.

This pack guide is, in essence, a map. A written map, if you will, to some of the best Nature has to offer. There are few other places on Earth that offer the rich diversity of outdoor terrain, wildlife, and life-changing adventures found around Estes Park, Colorado—the gateway to Rocky Mountain National Park. As a visitor, you'll have access to numerous trails, quiet alpine lakes, cold tumbling streams, and magnificent peaks. You'll also have proximity to a wide variety of wildlife, including yellow-bellied marmots, elk, bighorn sheep, black bear, moose, and, one of my favorites, the diminutive but talkative pika.

I wanted to help create this pack guide because I want as many people as possible to experience the benefits and joys of active travel in the great outdoors, particularly in the Estes Park area—only an hour's drive from my home in Fort Collins.

Since 1987 I've been designing and leading small-group adventures for folks 50 and better in more than 30 destinations around the world. As a guide, safety is my number one priority on all trips, for all travelers. This is my highest priority for you as well. Please keep in mind that while Nature holds great beauty, and—on clear, sunny days—can appear benign, having the proper clothing and gear, carrying enough food and drink, and understanding the ever-changing nature of weather in the mountains are absolutely essential to safe outdoor travel.

While listing everything one might need for safe travel in the mountains is not within the purview of this book, this guide does contain numerous resources to help you make good decisions on what to have with you on every hike. Don't skimp on the necessities. The Colorado Mountain Club offers numerous classes on safe travel in the outdoors. Contact them or peruse your favorite bookstore or library for books on this topic.

> **Caveat—on maps and map scales**
>
> In producing this pack guide, we have endeavored to provide the most accurate information possible. This striving for accuracy includes the map segments which follow each trail description. Many of the trails indicated by the red lines, however, include contours, ups and downs, and switchbacks that cannot be depicted on a small map. Thus, with some maps, you may find what looks like a variance between the stated length of the trail and the length of the trail when compared to the scale indicator.
>
> For every trail described in this guide, we list relevant, larger-scale maps of the area you will be hiking in—such as Trails Illustrated and USGS maps. It is always a good practice to secure these larger maps, study them, and understand where the smaller map from the guide fits within the larger map. The best practice is to carry both maps on your hike.

And, please, always remember that our outdoor environments are fragile; we are the keepers of our outdoor heritage. Follow the guidelines for minimum-impact travel. Too often, I see visitors gleefully feeding chipmunks and ground squirrels while sitting directly in front of a "Do Not Feed the Wildlife" sign. But that's not for you and me—we don't feed the wildlife ever, nor do we disturb them in their habitat or disrupt their activities.

Use this guide to find great beauty and adventure, but use good common sense and caution when deciding when and where to travel. Plan your hikes with safety in mind, so you can happily return again and again.

In adventure,
Ward Luthi

The Ten Essentials Systems

This pack guide is published by the Colorado Mountain Club—now in its 101st year of fostering safe practices and environmental stewardship in the wild areas of our state. Every hiker—experienced or beginner—will benefit by studying these principles, practicing them, and teaching them to others.

Read carefully—these are the items you really want to carry:

1. **Hydration.** Each day hiker should carry a minimum of two quarts, or liters, of water. In more arid regions, carry more. A good practice is to have lots of extra water in your vehicle—drink a good deal of it before setting out, and save some for the end of your experience. Consider purchasing a CamelBak® or similar soft carrier that fits inside of, or attached to, your daypack—having a drinking tube close to your face while you are hiking is a great way to stay hydrated. Whatever you do, continue drinking while you are on the trail—if you wait until you are thirsty, you've waited too long.

2. **Nutrition.** Don't skimp on ingesting energy-producing foods. Eat a large and healthy breakfast before hiking. Pack a good lunch with lots of fruits, vegetables, and carbohydrates. Carry quick energy snacks such as trail mix and nutrition bars—as much as anything this can help keep your mind clear for decision making.

3. **Sun protection.** Apply—and re-apply—sunscreen with at least a 45 SPF rating. Apply lip balm. Wear sunglasses and a wide-brimmed hat. Keep in mind that the sun's UV rays at 10,000 feet are roughly 25 percent stronger than at sea level, and if you are around snow, as much as 90 percent of the sunlight is reflected back a second time.

4. **Insulation.** Carry extra clothing to fit different critical needs. Colorado's weather can change in very short intervals; be prepared to cope with nature's surprises. More than anything else, you want to stay warm and dry, so pack accordingly. Cotton is the serious enemy here, leave it home; wool and synthetic materials will serve you well. Layering is critical, especially in cold or wet weather; put clothing on or take it off as the situation changes. Hypothermia—a potentially life-threatening decrease in body temperature—is most active at the top of your head. Carry a warm hat, warm gloves, and an extra pair of socks. Be prepared for wet weather with a parka or shell and rain pants. Experienced hikers will spend the little extra time needed to make clothing changes as often as their situation requires.

5. **Navigation.** Basic route-finding abilities are a critical skill for all hikers, even on what seem to be clearly marked trails. Learn minimal proficiency with a map and compass. Before you hike, use a map of the entire area and study your route. A global positioning system (GPS) device can add to your capabilities.

6. **Illumination.** A flashlight, with extra batteries, is an essential part of your gear. A better idea is to carry a headlamp, which allows both hands to be free. Nighttime hiking can be hazardous; avoid it except in emergencies.

7. **First Aid.** There are good hiker's first aid kits available or you can create one that best fits your needs and preferences. Consider including:
   - A plastic container of alcohol and/or hydrogen peroxide—useful for cleaning a wound, dealing with insect bites, etc.
   - A bandana—has many uses, including as an arm sling or emergency tourniquet

Beaver on lunch break.

- Duct tape—can go over a blister or wound, provide emergency repairs, and serve many other uses
- Hygiene supplies—liquid soap, latex gloves, toilet paper, and Ziploc bags—nothing is left in the woods
- A chart or booklet on how to deal with medical emergencies

8. **Fire.** Open fires in the woods should be considered dangerous and avoided when at all possible. If emergency circumstances force you to build an open fire—for warmth or cooking—use all possible care. Carry fire ribbon or waterproof matches in a watertight container. Hardened tree sap and dry pine needles can help get a fire going. If you will be cooking on the trail, use a hiker's portable stove and fuel in a very tight metal container.

9. **Repair kit and emergency tools.** Carry a small pocket knife or, better, a multi-use tool with a decent blade. Duct tape and electrical tape can serve many purposes. Carry a signal mirror and whistle in your tool kit.

10. **Emergency shelter.** Carry some nylon cord and a space blanket or a bivouac sack. A large plastic leaf

bag can have multiple uses—temporary rain shelter, a cover for your pack, or a survival shelter. Use the bag on your way out to carry trash left behind by less thoughtful hikers.

OTHER USEFUL SAFETY MEASURES

Tell someone where you'll be hiking and when you plan to return.

Leave a note on your dashboard, readable from outside your vehicle, that provides information about your hike—where you are heading, when you will return, how many are in your party, and contact information for family or friends.

Carry a SPOT—this satellite-activated personal locator can tell emergency personnel that you need help and where to find you. These devices retail for around $100 or more, but can save lives. When you're not hiking, keep the device in your vehicle for emergency use.

A NOTE ON HYPOTHERMIA

This is the phenomenon where wetness or cold, or a combination of the two, chills the body and results in a lowering of its core temperature. When not addressed, hypothermia can be fatal. Water is the severest conductor of heat loss and more cases of hypothermia have been recorded in the summer than in the winter. Cotton is considered a killer—it retains water and chills the body. Wool and synthetics tend to wick the water away and can retain heat even when damp. Gear up at the first sign of rain; change out of wet clothes at the first opportunity.

LEAVE NO TRACE

Trashing wild places is not an option: if you pack it in, pack it out—leave only footprints:

- Plan ahead and prepare for the cleanest possible adventure.

- Stay on the trail and don't shortcut on switchbacks; camp on durable surfaces, such as rock or sand. Above timberline, hike on rocks and avoid damaging the tundra. When more than one person is off trail, spread out so you don't start destructive new "social" trails.
- Dispose of all waste properly, including that deposited by your dog. Pack it in, pack it out.
- Leave what you find—look at it, take a photo, and leave it for the next person.
- Minimize campfire impacts—think small, keep the fuel within the fire circle, and unless it is a permanent fire pit, destroy all traces of your fire before leaving your campsite. Forest fires have started from small campfires; be extremely cautious in this regard.
- Respect wildlife—don't feed them anything and don't intrude on their feeding and breeding areas. Moose deserve your complete respect; they are considered the most dangerous creatures in the Colorado woods.
- Be considerate of animals and other humans in the woods—no radios or other unnecessary noise. Part of the lure of the woods is the healing sound of wind through the trees, the murmur of a stream, or no noise at all.

Another good map source...

In producing this and other pack guides, we frequently refer to Trails Illustrated™ and USGS maps as reliable reference sources.

In preparing *The Best Estes Park Hikes* and *The Best Rocky Mountain National Park Hikes*, we've also employed with satisfaction three maps produced by regional outdoor author and cartographer Raymond Ave. There is an Eastern RMNP and a Western RMNP version and a "full coverage" RMNP map.

Ave's maps are available at the RMNP Visitors' Center and regional retail outdoor shops and bookstores in Estes Park, Fort Collins, Grand Lake, and elsewhere.

1. Balanced Rock

BY KURT WORRELL

MAPS	Trails Illustrated, Rocky Mountain National Park, Number 200 USGS, Estes Park Quadrangle 7.5 Minute
ELEVATION GAIN	1,638 feet
RATING	Moderate
ROUND-TRIP DISTANCE	7.8 miles
ROUND-TRIP TIME	4 hours
NEAREST LANDMARK	Estes Park

COMMENT: Lumpy Ridge, your access to Balanced Rock, is a prominent feature of Rocky Mountain National Park. Just north of Estes Park, it is visible from all portions of the Estes Valley. It is located on Devils Gulch Road and gives you a lightly traveled path through Glen Haven and back to US 34 near Drake. Lumpy Ridge is home to rock formations that are favorite destinations for technical rock climbers. This hike, along with others in the area, offers vantage points for over 100 published rock climbing routes on the ridge.

Although part of RMNP, access to the Lumpy Ridge trailhead does not require any permits or RMNP entry fees. This modern trailhead replaces the Twin Owl and Gem Lake trailheads, sports a generous number of parking spots, and is equipped with toilets. The convenient access from Estes Park makes this a popular destination for all levels of outdoor enthusiast. An early start is recommended in order to secure a parking spot, avoid the foot traffic in the first half of the hike, and beat the afternoon heat you may encounter on this south-facing trail. Water is not available at the trailhead.

Balanced Rock's namesake.   PHOTO BY MARLENE BORNEMAN

The trail climbs along and through the various lumps that make up the namesake ridge, passing steep and rocky terrain initially, and riparian timber forest nearer Balanced Rock. The trails are well groomed and easily passable with light duty hiking gear. Past Gem Lake, the trail gives a glimpse of the full lifecycle of a pine forest, revealing new growth closely contrasted with trees suffering from pine beetle infestation and those that have died from high winds, fire, and other natural causes.

The trail passes through chipmunk habitat but is also a passageway for mountain lions to traverse from the Estes Valley back to the high country, and group travel is recommended. The views along the first 2 miles of the trail offer spectacular landscapes, with Estes Park in the foreground, the Front Range peaks as your backdrop, and the diamond face of Longs Peak as the centerpiece. Closer to Balanced Rock, the more isolated Mummy Range peaks are visible to the northwest.

For extra credit, watch for naturally occurring holes through various boulders along the trail. One is 10" in diameter while others are about the size of your hand. You should be able to find at least four without leaving the trail, plus one easily visible rock with two such holes just past Gem Lake.

GETTING THERE: From the intersection of US 36 and US 34 in the heart of Estes Park, travel 0.3 mile on US 34 (West Wonderview Avenue) past the historic Stanley Hotel to MacGregor Avenue. Turn right (north) and drive 0.7 mile north on MacGregor Avenue and follow the road as it turns sharply eastward and the name changes to Devils Gulch Road. Continue 0.5 mile and turn left onto Lumpy Ridge Road at the well-marked sign to the Lumpy Ridge trailhead. The parking lot is 0.3 mile north and is configured as a one-way loop cul-de-sac.

THE ROUTE: At the Lumpy Ridge trailhead, two trails are available: Twin Owls to the west and Gem Lake to the east. The distance from this point to Gem Lake is 1.7 miles. Follow the Gem Lake Trail eastward and pass through a wooden access control gate/fence roughly 100 yards from the trailhead. At this point the well-constructed trail turns northward and heads 0.5 mile at a roughly 16 percent grade, passing through typical Colorado pine forest. The views of the namesake lumpy rock outcroppings and pillars are numerous. Keep an eye out for the technical rock climbers on the vertical rock formations.

At 0.5 mile, a signpost marks the junction to the loop trail. Continue right (east) toward Gem Lake on a much more moderate trail meandering along Lumpy Ridge. In 0.75 mile

Balanced Flake, a curious rock structure, but not your destination.

PHOTO BY KURT WORRELL

note the large boot-shaped rock, colloquially known as Paul Bunyan's Boot, on the left at a pair of sharp but short switchbacks. If the trail is kicking your butt, this may be a good spot for a photograph. Continue on the trail, and it soon will present an alternate path (rejoining 10 yards up the trail) for the adventuresome to travel through a short rock tunnel. By this point, the trail grade has increased to an average of 20 percent and will continue with switchbacks until you reach the privy and, 0.1 mile later, arrive at Gem Lake.

Upon arriving at Gem Lake, follow the trail along the north shore of the lake and exit from the enclosing rock formation heading to the northeast. A sign marks the distance from this point to Balanced Rock as 2.1 miles.

The trail descends through a well-shaded aspen grove for roughly 0.3 mile and continues to gradually descend for another 0.5 mile through pine forest more common to the high altitude Colorado area. The trail meanders north and eastward near the edge of Lumpy Ridge—where photo opportunities abound. It eventually turns northwest and skirts the base of the steep eastern edge gemstones to a junction with the Cow Creek Trail.

The signpost at the junction pulls you deeper into the open forest toward Balanced Rock, continuing west for a time on mostly flat to gradually rising terrain, as the northern extent of the gemstones are rounded. The trail then descends briefly into the neighboring valley and travels along the eastern valley wall to the bottom. Near the bottom you will see the possibly confusing—and false—destination depicted in the photo as Balanced Flake. The trail follows the bottom of the valley southward toward the back side of Lumpy Ridge.

As the valley end nears, the trail ascends, and then descends a few hundred feet, revealing Balanced Rock directly ahead and at the end of the trail. With a little bouldering effort, you can reach the underside of the Balanced Rock. Be mindful of the 30-foot drop on the north side of the rock formation. On the return hike, several westerly oriented rock viewpoints can be reached, with alternate views of the Balanced Rock. Return to Gem Lake by retracing the same trail.

TRAILHEAD

2. Bridal Veil Falls

BY SALLIE VARNER

MAP	Trails Illustrated, Rocky Mountain National Park, Number 200
ELEVATION GAIN	1,000 feet
RATING	Moderate
ROUND-TRIP DISTANCE	6.25 miles
ROUND-TRIP TIME	4–5 hours
NEAREST LANDMARK	MacGregor Avenue (a/k/a Devils Gulch Road)

COMMENT: Bridal Veil Falls are thought by some to be among the prettiest waterfalls in Rocky Mountain National Park. They are also easily accessible, making them a popular destination for many hikers. Because of its relatively low elevation, this is a good year-round hike.

The hike to Bridal Veil Falls starts at the historic McGraw Ranch. The ranch, which dates back to 1884, started as a cattle ranch but eventually was converted to a guest ranch that was operated successfully for several decades. The National Park Service acquired the ranch in 1988, and it is now operated as the McGraw Ranch Research Center.

GETTING THERE: From the junction of US 34 and US 36 on the east side of Estes Park, take the US 34 bypass (Wonderview Ave.) for about 0.5 mile, past the Safeway and the Stanley Hotel. Turn right onto MacGregor Avenue (Devils Gulch Road) and drive north and east for 3.5 miles to the well-signed McGraw Ranch Road. Turn left onto McGraw Ranch Road and drive 2 miles on the good dirt road to reach the roadside parking for the Cow Creek trailhead. Trailhead parking is parallel along the west side of the road. Parking spaces are limited

Bridal Veil Falls—worth the hike.   PHOTO BY SALLIE VARNER

and may become filled during summer weekends; there is no easily accessible place for overflow parking. Rocky Mountain National Park has placed an LED sign at the start of McGraw Ranch Road to let visitors know when the lot is full. The trailhead has a pit toilet and trash cans.

Access to both Rocky Mountain National Park and Comanche Peak Wilderness Area trails is available through McGraw Ranch. Walk to the end of the road at the bottom of the hill. Cross the bridge and pass around the gate. The road through the ranch buildings curves to the left. The toilet is located about 0.25 mile from the gate, on the west side of the McGraw Ranch buildings.

THE ROUTE: After passing through McGraw Ranch, the route follows the ranch road until it fades into a trail after 0.65 mile. Continue west along the good trail as it climbs easily, following Cow Creek on the left. This is a good area to spot wildlife—deer, coyotes, and wild turkeys are frequent visitors.

Another small falls along the way.

PHOTO BY SALLIE VARNER

At 1.2 miles, reach the junction with the trail to Balanced Rock and Gem Lake. The turnoff for the Rabbit Ears campsite is reached shortly after the Gem Lake junction. The Rabbit Ears is a unique rock formation located on the ridge just above the campsite. You can't see the rock formation at this point on the trail, but keep on toward Bridal Veil Falls for another 0.25 mile or so, then look back and up and the formation is very obvious.

The junction of Cow Creek and Dark Canyon trails is reached 2 miles into the hike. The left fork is the Dark Canyon Trail, which continues to the west. For Bridal Veil Falls, take the right fork to head northwest, still following Cow Creek.

The trail now begins to climb somewhat more steeply. As you climb, the canyon narrows and becomes more rocky, rugged, and dramatic. Watch for interesting rock formations—beautiful to look at and fun for scrambling. The trail follows the creek much more closely, as it flows over many small drops, slides, and falls. As it climbs higher, the trail gets increasingly rockier, eventually crossing large rock faces and climbing crude rock steps. This final part of the hike has the potential to be treacherous if the conditions are wet or icy. A little over 1.0 mile from the Dark Canyon junction, reach Bridal Veil Falls at the head of the canyon. To return, retrace your steps to the trailhead.

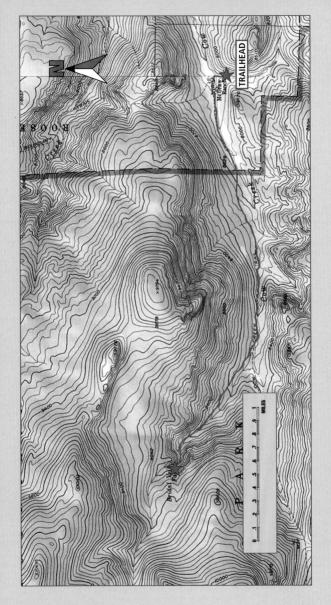

TRAILHEAD

McGraw
Ranch

ROOSE

BOUNDARY

CREEK

x 8857

x 9794

x 9738

Bridal Veil
Fall

P A R K

MILES
0 .1 .2 .3 .4 .5 .6 .7 .8 .9 1

3. Emerald Mountain

BY NATHANIEL POTSON

MAPS	Trails Illustrated, Rocky Mountain National Park, Number 200 USGS, Longs Peak Quadrangle 7.5 Minute
ELEVATION GAIN	519 feet
RATING	Easy–moderate
ROUND-TRIP DISTANCE	1.8 miles
ROUND-TRIP TIME	Under 2 hours
NEAREST LANDMARK	Estes Park

COMMENT: Emerald Mountain is located along the eastern edge of Rocky Mountain National Park (RMNP) at the end of Colorado 66. The mountain's striking feature, in terms of location, is its situation between Glacier Basin and the famous YMCA of the Rockies.

While the mountain is accessible from all three of these locations—Glacier Basin, the Emerald Mountain trailhead, and the YMCA of the Rockies—thoughtful hikers proceed with caution. While the majority of the mountain is under public ownership, some of the land is privately held and should be respected. It is recommended that the East Portal trailhead be your access point.

The final destination, and much of the trail that can be used, is visible from where you park your car. What makes this hike a delight is how much can be accomplished over a short distance. Be aware, though, that while the distance is short, the mountain can provide a challenging change in altitude.

Emerald Mountain gets its name from its coniferous northern slope that faces the YMCA. On the sunnier southern slope, the hiker is faced with a dryer climate and little shade,

Front Range vista from Emerald Mountain Trail.   PHOTO BY NATHANIEL POTSON

but the wildflowers that can be found along this montane meadow more than make up for it—not to mention the view from the top.

Views from the summit of Emerald Peak are impressive. A survey of your surroundings will show much of the Front Range, including Longs Peak—the highest peak in the park and a clearly dominating presence to the south. You will also see the "tops" of Notchtop, Knobtop, and Gabletop forming a wall to the west. Thunder and Lightning peaks, unofficially named, appear as cones to the south, while the snowcapped Mummy Range is visible to the north. Although a short hike, Emerald Peak has much to offer.

GETTING THERE: From Estes Park, go west along US 36 until it intersects with Hwy 66, heading southwesterly. There you will see a sign that directs you to either RMNP or the YMCA (the highway junction of 66/698). Turn left towards the YMCA; this junction is clearly signed, indicating the YMCA to the left and RMNP to the right. You will go past the YMCA on your right and continue along 66 until the road becomes a parking loop at the East Portal campground. It is possible to park in the loop outside the campground. The overall drive is about 4.2 miles from downtown Estes Park.

Rock cairns mark the route to the summit. PHOTO BY NATHANIEL POTSON

THE ROUTE: To reach the trail, walk past the East Portal campground towards the East Portal trailhead. On the way, there is a gate that limits vehicle access to the eastern terminus of the Alva Adams Tunnel. A small holding pond marks the route up to the trail. At this point, you will know you are on the correct route. Now head uphill to the trail. Here the trail is unmarked, but you will be able to note the beginning of the trail, because there is a horse hitching rack directly in front of the trail, which somewhat obscures the immediate view of the trail.

The majority of your route is visible because it continuously leads uphill and eventually will be signed as the Wind River Trail.

Continue up the trail for approximately another 0.1 mile. Directly next to the trail, and continuing to the top of Emerald Mountain, is a large rock outcropping, with cairns indicating a lightly used or sometimes obscure trail. Pay careful attention in order not to miss these cairns. If you reach a grove of aspen trees, you will have missed the cairn outcropping and gone too far.

This trail, while not well worn, will lead to the top of the mountain. It will pass through a meadow, but foliage returns as you near the summit. You will reach a large outcropping that appears to be the summit, but this actually marks a false summit. You are, however, close to the true summit. You'll know you've reached the actual summit when an almost complete 360-degree view is attained, with a clear view of both the Front Range and the Mummy Range. Although most of the hike is below tree level, the vista from this opening at the top makes your effort worthwhile.

Return to the trailhead by retracing your steps.

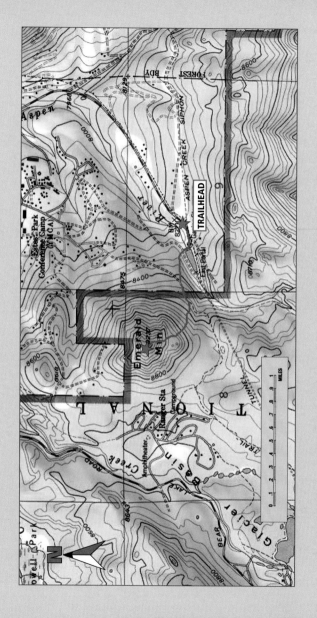

4. Estes Cone Trail

BY CAROLINE BLACKWELL SCHMIEDT

MAPS	Trails Illustrated, Rocky Mountain National Park, Number 200 USGS, Estes Park Quadrangle 7.5 minute
ELEVATION GAIN	2,391 feet
RATING	Moderate
ROUND-TRIP DISTANCE	6.8 miles
ROUND-TRIP TIME	5.0 hours
NEAREST LANDMARK	Estes Park

COMMENT: The summit of Estes Cone offers some of the best views found anywhere in Rocky Mountain National Park. While getting there takes some effort, those who climb Estes Cone are rewarded with a 360-degree view encompassing the Estes Valley, Mummy Range, Continental Divide, Longs Peak, Mount Meeker, Twin Sisters, and Lily Lake below. The summit area is fairly small, with a significant amount of exposure, and may not be suitable for younger children or inexperienced hikers. Reaching the summit requires some fun rock scrambling. This is a classic Colorado climb, and for most folks, is not to be missed.

Estes Cone is accessed from Storm Pass. Most hikers choose one of two routes to reach Storm Pass. The first begins at the Longs Peak trailhead and passes by the Eugenia Mine. Evidence of a log cabin at the mine site provides some nice photo opportunities. This route is especially popular as a snowshoe trail in winter. A second and slightly longer route begins at the Lily Lake parking area. This route, described below, provides wonderful views of Longs Peak and Mount Meeker as it approaches Storm Pass.

Longs Peak and Mount Meeker from Estes Cone.

From Storm Pass, the Estes Cone Trail climbs steeply through a boulder field. Here a forest of short, twisted pines thrives in the harsh and windswept environment.

GETTING THERE: From the junction of US 36 and Colorado 7 in Estes Park, on the south side of Lake Estes, drive south on Colorado 7 for 6.3 miles to the Lily Lake parking area on the right. To access the trailhead from the south, drive roughly 10 miles north of Allenspark on Colorado 7.

THE ROUTE: The trailhead is located on the south side of the Lily Lake parking lot. Stop here for a moment to take a look at the Lily Lake kiosk. The trail begins behind this kiosk and travels south along a gravel road. Follow the signs to Storm Pass. After a few hundred yards, the trail veers to the right, leaving the road and entering the forest.

Once in the forest, the trail descends to a wooden bridge over Aspen Brook. From the bridge, the trail climbs steadily to the northwest, providing good views of Lily Mountain.

Within 1.0 mile, the trail switchbacks to the southwest and continues climbing steadily through a forest of lodgepole pines. The trail then contours around Estes Cone on its

Yes, it's *this* trail.   PHOTO BY WARD LUTHI

southeast flank. Here there are good views of Twin Sisters, to the southeast.

As the trail continues along the south flank of Estes Cone and begins to level out, look for a short side trail on the left. This sandy trail leads to an overlook providing nice views to the south and a view to the northwest of the summit towering above.

The trail continues along the south flank of Estes Cone to Storm Pass, offering wonderful views of Longs Peak and Mount Meeker to the south. At Storm Pass you will find a large cairn and a few directional signs. This is a good place to rest, have a snack, and drink some water. You will need energy for the work ahead. Turn right at Storm Pass and follow the cairns. Here the trail enters a boulder field and switchbacks multiple times as it climbs steeply through a forest of short, twisted pines.

Once you have reached the summit area, continue following the cairns eastward to a rocky gully sloping sharply upward and hugging a rock cliff. The base of this gully is a good place to leave your hiking poles, because you will need your hands to climb here. Scramble up this gully and continue following cairns eastward for a very short distance. Do not descend too far. From here, another short scramble puts you on the summit. Return to the trailhead by retracing your steps.

TRAILHEAD

5. Eugenia Mine Trail

BY SALLIE VARNER

MAPS	Trails Illustrated, Rocky Mountain National Park, Number 200 USGS, Longs Peak Quadrangle 7.5 minute
ELEVATION GAIN	500 feet
RATING	Easy
ROUND-TRIP DISTANCE	2.7 miles
ROUND-TRIP TIME	2–3 hours
NEAREST LANDMARK	Colorado 7

COMMENT: The Eugenia Mine is situated on Inn Brook near the base of Battle Mountain, a 12,044-foot neighbor of Longs Peak. The mine was staked in 1905 by Carl Norwell and Edward Cudahy, in the hopes of striking a rich gold vein. Norwell and Cudahy invested considerable time, effort, and resources in the mine, including tunneling 1,000 feet into the mountain and installing a small rail system to carry ore. Despite their optimism and hard work, the mine was never a big producer.

When the Eugenia Mine was claimed, it lay in what is today part of Wyoming's Medicine Bow National Forest, which at that time extended south into northern Colorado. The bill designating Rocky Mountain National Park was signed into law by President Woodrow Wilson on January 26, 1915. The mine continued working for four years after its inclusion in the National Park, but was finally abandoned in 1919.

The hike to the Eugenia Mine site is a fun outing for all ages. The trail is short, without too much climbing, and offers intriguing glimpses of the south side of Estes Cone through the trees, the Tahosa Valley far below to the east,

Junction of Longs Peak and Eugenia Mine trails. PHOTO BY SALLIE VARNER

and Twin Sisters across the valley. In addition to building remains and a few other artifacts left from its mining days, the site is very pretty and offers an interesting glimpse into Colorado history.

GETTING THERE: From the junction of US 34 and US 36 on the east side of Estes Park, turn southeasterly onto US 36. Proceed for about 0.5 mile to the Y-junction with Colorado 7 and take the right fork onto Colorado 7. Drive south for 9 miles to Longs Peak Road, at mile marker 9. The Longs Peak Road turn-off is well marked, with a large sign saying "Longs Peak Area." Turn right onto Longs Peak Road and drive west—up the paved, winding road for 1.2 miles to the Longs Peak Trail parking area. The Longs Peak area is very popular and on summer weekends the parking lot may be full. If it is, parking is allowed on the narrow pull-offs on the side of the road leading to the parking area.

The parking area is well equipped, with flush toilets and running water (summer only) and vault toilets (off season); picnic tables; and trash and recycling bins. Also, there is a ranger station with informational displays and a very small gift shop.

A rusting relic of the Eugenia Mine.

PHOTO BY SALLIE VARNER

THE ROUTE: The hike to the Eugenia Mine site follows the Longs Peak Trail for approximately 0.5 mile. Starting from the parking lot, follow the wide, well-maintained trail as it climbs gradually toward the west. This is the main access point for climbing Longs Peak, and other destinations in the Longs Peak area, so this trail sees a lot of use throughout the year.

At about 0.5 mile, watch for the sign noting the turn-off for the Eugenia Mine Trail. The trail turns off to the right to head north toward the mine. While much of the elevation for this hike is gained during the first 0.5 mile, there are several ups and downs between the trail junction and the mine site. Glimpses of Estes Cone can be had through the trees to the north.

The Eugenia Mine is situated on Inn Brook and a low footbridge crosses the pretty brook just before the mine site. There are several small trails leading through the mine site, allowing visitors to explore the area. As with all natural and man-made features in the national park, please enjoy the Eugenia Mine site without disturbing or moving the federally protected remains.

From the Eugenia Mine, the trail continues north across Storm Pass and past Estes Cone to its northern terminus on the Bear Lake Road.

The return hike to the Longs Peak trailhead is surprisingly easy, considering the number of ups and downs encountered on the way to the mine. To return, retrace your steps to the trailhead.

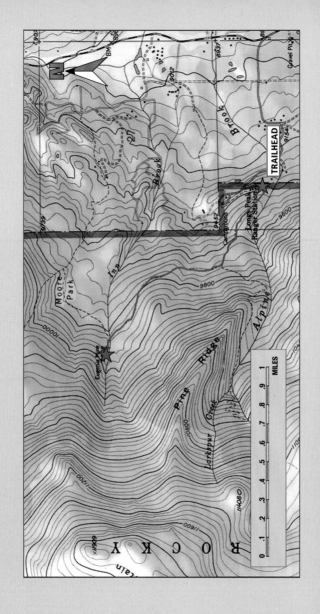

N

TRAILHEAD

Brook

Brook

Inn

Moore Park

Eugenia Mine

Pine Ridge

Alpine

Larkspur Creek

Longs Peak
Ranger Station

Campground

R O C K Y

Mountain

9937

9912

9739

9452

9600

9800

10000

10800

11600

11200

11400

9754

MILES

0 .1 .2 .3 .4 .5 .6 .7 .8 .9 1

6. Gem Lake Trail

BY CAROLINE BLACKWELL SCHMIEDT

MAPS	Trails Illustrated, Rocky Mountain National Park, Number 200, USGS, Estes Park Quadrangle 7.5 Minute
ELEVATION GAIN	968 feet
RATING	Easy–moderate
ROUND-TRIP DISTANCE	3.6 miles
ROUND-TRIP TIME	3.0 hours
NEAREST LANDMARK	Estes Park

COMMENT: The Gem Lake Trail is one of the best hikes in the Estes Park area. It is truly a "gem." What makes this hike one of the best? First, there are wonderful viewing spots along the way that will invite you to stop and enjoy panoramic scenes of high mountains. Closer to the lake, there is an interesting rock formation shaped like a boot with a hole in the bottom of it. This is a fun place to take some pictures. Second, Gem Lake has something to offer everyone. For families, it is a fairly short hike and is not too strenuous for school-aged children. For those with limited time, Gem Lake can be hiked in a few hours, yet it provides enough elevation gain to give you some exercise. Finally, the lake itself is beautiful. Steep granite cliffs tower over the lake on the east side, while its sandy beach on the north beckons children to take off their shoes and wade in the water.

Gem Lake can be hiked year round. The south facing trail receives enough sunshine to remain relatively snow free. Located in the Lumpy Ridge area, the trail is a showcase for weathered granite rock formations of all shapes and sizes. Every visitor will see something different in this unique environment.

Gem Lake—a true gem.   PHOTO BY JON QUEBBEMAN

My favorite time of year to hike Gem Lake is in the fall, when portions of the trail glow with yellow and gold aspen leaves. In places, the fallen leaves cover the trail completely in a blanket of color.

GETTING THERE: From the junction of US 34 and US 36 in Estes Park, continue a short distance west on US 34. Turn right on MacGregor Avenue and continue until it turns sharply to the right, becoming Devils Gulch Road. Follow Devils Gulch Road for 0.5 mile to the trailhead entrance on the left, marked by a brown sign. Turn left onto Lumpy Ridge Road and drive 500 yards to the parking area.

THE ROUTE: The trail begins on the north side of the parking lot next to a restroom facility. Walk a short distance east and weave your way through a fence. Stop here for a moment to look at the Gem Lake kiosk. Continue up the trail to the left. Be sure to stay on the trail here as it runs parallel to private property.

An unlikely rock formation. PHOTO BY CAROLINE BLACKWELL SCHMIEDT

The trail climbs steadily for the first 0.5 mile to the junction with the Twin Owls trail. At the junction, turn right and continue climbing. The trail soon levels out and becomes sandy. It also widens in this area and can be tricky to follow. Several side trails veer off to the right, leading to rocky outcrops providing panoramic views. These are worth exploring.

The trail continues climbing and soon reaches a flat granite outcrop that provides a wonderful place to rest and enjoy sweeping views of the Continental Divide, Longs Peak, Twin Sisters, and Estes Park below.

From the outcrop, the trail continues through the forest. A log bridge provides easy access across a small stream. From here the trail climbs steeply. Just before reaching the lake, the boot shaped rock outcrop provides a photo opportunity and perhaps some rock scrambling.

Continue climbing a short distance to the lake. For an added adventure, continue on to Balanced Rock (see description on page 20). To return, retrace your steps to the trailhead.

TRAILHEAD

MILES

0 .1 .2 .3 .4 .5 .6 .7 .8 .9 1

7. Homer Rouse Trail

BY JACK POWERS

MAPS	Trails Illustrated, Rocky Mountain National Park, Number 200 USGS, Longs Peak Quadrangle 7.5 Minute
ELEVATION GAIN	687 feet
RATING	Easy
ROUND-TRIP DISTANCE	3.6 miles
ROUND-TRIP TIME	80–100 minutes
NEAREST LANDMARK	Estes Park

COMMENT: The Homer Rouse Trail gently climbs from the pasturelands at the southeast edge of Estes Park to the parking area opposite Lily Lake. Most of the trail follows a road that had been the principal southern route out of Estes Park until it was replaced by Colorado 7. There is a short section of more conventional trail that bypasses private property.

The route was converted to a trail through the cooperative efforts of several agencies in Larimer County. It is named after Homer Rouse, who served as superintendent of Rocky Mountain National Park from 1992 to 1995. The route connects trails in Estes Park to trails in Rocky Mountain National Park.

Aspens line the route for much of its distance, especially along the lower portions. Their golden fall display, with mountains looming in the background, could be a delight for photographers. Conifers are more predominant in the higher sections. The route also goes past the historic Baldpate Inn, which was built in 1917.

Some trail guides suggest that the trail starts at the parking lot at the junction of Fish Creek Way and Fish Creek

On the trail again.   PHOTO BY JACK POWERS

Road. Trails Illustrated maps show the trail starting at the point where the gravel road turns east to the Cheley Camp. In this book, the round-trip distance, elevation gain, and round-trip estimated time are based on the Trails Illustrated depiction and do not include the 0.5 miles from the parking lot.

GETTING THERE: To reach the south (higher elevation) trailhead from Estes Park, turn south on Colorado 7 at its junction with US 36. Drive roughly 6.3 miles south. The trailhead will be on the left (east) side of the road. The highway sign will identify it as the turn for Twin Sisters. The trail starts at the north end of the parking lot.

To reach the north (lower elevation) trailhead from Estes Park, turn south on Colorado 7 at its junction with US 36. Drive about 3.9 miles and turn left (east) onto Fish Creek Way, which is immediately past Grey Fox Drive on a sharp curve. (Note: Fish Creek Way is only 0.25 mile long and connects Colorado 7 to Fish Creek Road. There is no mention of Fish Creek Road as you drive along

The Baldpate Inn, a local landmark.

PHOTO BY JACK POWERS

Colorado 7.) Drive a little less than 0.25 mile and turn right, onto a gravel road. You will immediately see a parking lot on the left. You may park there and walk 0.5 mile to the start of the Homer Rouse Trail, as it is shown on the Trails Illustrated map. A sign marks the beginning of the trail, which continues straight south, while the main gravel road turns left towards the Cheley Camp. Alternately, you may drive up to that curve, park on the side of the road (where it is not prohibited), and access the trail from there.

THE ROUTE: The north (low) end of the trail is at the point where the gravel road turns east to the Cheley Camp. The hiking trail continues straight south, past a farm on the east side and a small log cabin on the west side. After 0.25 mile, the trail avoids private property by leaving the road and turning left into the woods. This section is a more conventional narrow path winding uphill. It is only a few hundred yards long and rejoins the dirt road just beyond a barricade on the road.

The road continues upward through aspens and conifers and passes the Baldpate Inn about 350 yards from the southern end of the trail. The trail ends at the parking lot opposite Lily Lake. The hiker who wants to add more miles can cross Colorado Route 7 to Lily Lake. (Use caution here as cars have the right of way.) You could also continue up the Twin Sisters Trail. Return to the trailhead by retracing your steps.

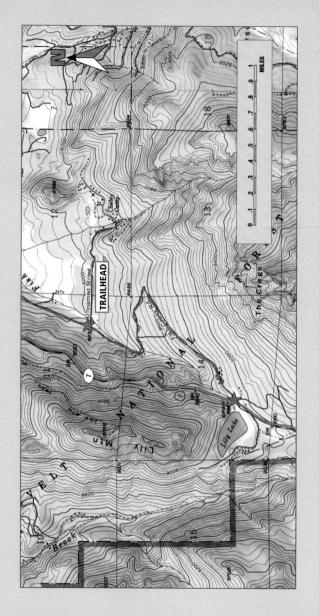

TRAILHEAD

MILES

8. Lake Estes Trail

BY AMY CROW

MAPS	Trails Illustrated, Rocky Mountain National Park, Number 200 Any map depicting the City of Estes Park
ELEVATION GAIN	None
RATING	Easy—handicapped accessible
ROUND-TRIP DISTANCE	3.75 miles
ROUND-TRIP TIME	1.5 hours
NEAREST LANDMARK	Estes Park

COMMENT: Lake Estes is the centerpiece of the Estes Valley, which has attracted visitors from around the world for more than 150 years. One only needs to view the valley from several vantage points to be in awe of this magical and majestic masterpiece of nature. Early prospectors and more recent travelers have stood speechless as they took in these shining mountains, which feature Longs Peak—one of the state's 54 peaks above 14,000 feet—the multi-tiered Mummy Range, and the geologic wonder of Lumpy Ridge.

Lake Estes is a relative newcomer to the valley—created in 1948, when Olympus Dam harnessed the Big Thompson River to create a water supply for points east. A trail was recently constructed, circumventing the entire lake, for the enjoyment of both local residents and visitors.

A pleasant walking excursion around Lake Estes offers, at every vantage point, a view of all the grandeur that is this valley. Many benches are available for visitors to rest on while they enjoy the panorama.

The trail provides a treat for all ages and abilities and the family pet, leashed, is welcome to use it. Points of interest include bird sanctuaries, wildflowers, and elk and other

Lake Estes with the Stanley Hotel on the hillside.   PHOTO BY AMY CROW

wildlife sightings. Your in-town adventure can include bridges across the tranquil Big Thompson River, fishing, boating, and bicycle rentals. The trail features a fishing pier designed for handicapped access.

GETTING THERE: Take US 34 from the Loveland/Fort Collins area, or US 36 through Lyons. Where these two highways intersect, park at the Estes Park Visitor Center, located on the southeast corner. A bridge leads to the lake loop. An additional entrance, off of US 36, leads to a picnic and fishing area, where a fee is required. Access is also available, free of charge, at the marina on the east side.

THE ROUTE: After crossing the Big Thompson River at the visitor center, the trail splits. A clockwise direction takes you to a bird sanctuary and the borders of the golf course. Consider making a daybreak start on the trail, when you

Exploring the Lake Estes Trail.

can expect less traffic on the path and you have an excellent chance to view wildlife. Similarly, during an evening stroll, the hiker is likely to see elk on the lake banks while also being treated to an abundant variety of birds and water fowl.

As the trail serpentines, Longs Peak and Mount Meeker come into view to the west. Lake Estes is bordered by private property and the trail soon passes by the Estes Park Resort and the Lake Estes Marina, where a variety of land and water vehicles are available for rent. From here, with Mount Olympus in the background, the trail loops around the dam before traveling along the west side of the lake. You'll see fishermen dotting the landscape—which includes large picnic areas complete with great views of the Mummy Mountains and Lumpy Ridge. In this area, another spur of the trail crosses under US 36 and features a lakeside dog park.

The trail is boldly marked with mileage markers along the path and is easy to follow around the Estes Park power plant before you head back to the starting point.

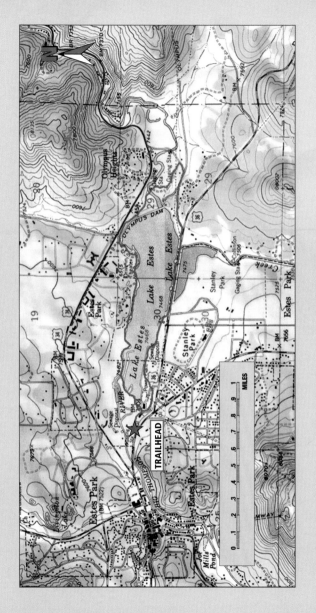

9. Lily Lake Trail

BY JACK POWERS

MAPS	Trails Illustrated, Rocky Mountain National Park, Number 200 USGS, Longs Peak Quadrangle 7.5 Minute
ELEVATION GAIN	None
RATING	Easy
ROUND-TRIP DISTANCE	0.8 miles
ROUND-TRIP TIME	15–30 minutes
NEAREST LANDMARK	Estes Park

COMMENT: The road from Estes Park to Lily Lake climbs 1,400 feet. This could suggest that you are driving into the heart of the mountains. That is true, but it is a heart with a lake at its center. That is the charm of this location.

The Lily Lake Trail itself is wide and flat with virtually no elevation gain. It is a trail that can be enjoyed by the very young, the elderly, and all ages in between. The fine gravel path is wheelchair accessible and individuals using wheelchairs can self-propel themselves over much of the trail. However, environmental factors can make parts of the trail more difficult, so it is prudent for those in a wheelchair not to go out alone in case the trail becomes impassable for them.

There are three picnic tables at the trailhead. A side trail on the south side of the lake leads to a picnic area that can be reserved for group activities. Catch and release fishing is also allowed at the lake.

The trail is best walked slowly; there is no need to hurry to a destination. The trail and lake are the destination, and walking the trail is a relaxing experience. The soothing effect of the water is amplified by the picturesque peaks

Lily Mountain reflections.

on the horizon in all directions. Benches are strategically placed so that you can stop and admire a particularly pleasing view.

Children in a certain age group have a limited tolerance for serenity. The Lily Ridge Trail, which parallels the lake on the north side, is a good vehicle for them to expend their pent-up energy. The trail is 0.7 mile long with elevation gain of a little over 100 feet. There are many steps, especially on the east side of the trail, so the Lily Ridge Trail is not recommended for those with joint or cardiovascular problems.

An evening visit to Lily Lake is a good option for those who arrive in town too late for more ambitious hikes. Likewise, those who want to do something other than stare at motel walls after dinner should consider a photo hike here in the evening sun.

GETTING THERE: From the east side of Estes Park, turn south on Colorado 7 at its junction with US 36. Drive roughly 6.33

Accessible trail at Lily Lake.   PHOTO BY JACK POWERS

miles south. The Lily Lake trailhead will be on the right (west) side of the road and nearly opposite the parking lot for the Twin Sisters and Homer Rouse trails. The parking lot on the east side can be used for overflow.

If you are coming from the south, the trailhead is roughly 13 miles from the junction of Colorado 7 and Colorado 72 and will be on the left (west) side of the road.

THE ROUTE: The trail starts and ends immediately next to the parking lot. There are three picnic tables at this spot. The trail is 4.0 to 6.5 feet wide, with a fine gravel surface. Log curbs line both sides of the trail along the entire route. This prevents strollers and wheelchairs from going off the trail.

The trail stays close to the lake, sometimes at its very edge. There are many benches along the trail, giving the weary a chance to take a break and allowing others to simply sit and enjoy the view. There are more benches on the south side of the lake, perhaps because the views of Estes Cone, Mount Meeker, and Longs Peak are more popular.

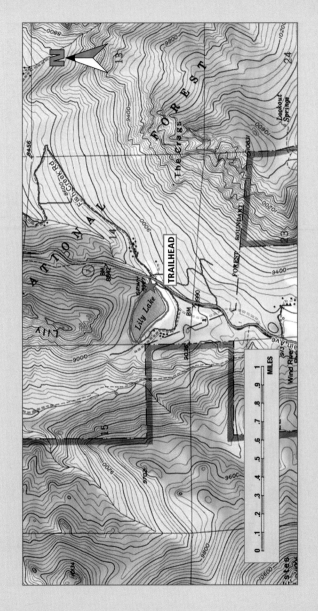

10. Lily Mountain Trail

BY JACK POWERS

MAPS	Trails Illustrated, Rocky Mountain National Park, Number 200 USGS, Longs Peak Quadrangle 7.5 minute
ELEVATION GAIN	1,000 feet
RATING	Moderate
ROUND-TRIP DISTANCE	3.8 miles
ROUND-TRIP TIME	2.5 hours
NEAREST LANDMARK	Estes Park

COMMENT: Lily Mountain is immediately north of Lily Lake. The peak is less than 10,000 feet high, which makes it lower than such neighbors as Twin Sisters and Estes Cone. This in no way diminishes the grandeur of the scenery along the trail.

Twin Sisters lies in full view to the east. Looking northeast, the hiker can enjoy wide views of the meadows north of Estes Park, with glimpses of Lake Estes. Lumpy Ridge, the Mummy Range, and the town of Estes Park itself are laid out below as the trail reaches its northern limit. Views from the summit include the peaks of the Continental Divide, Estes Cone, Mount Meeker, and Longs Peak.

The trail is fairly level on the section heading north; much of the total elevation gain is crammed into the last 0.7 mile. The very last section of trail is about 70 yards of steep scramble over boulders. Those who do reach the summit are rewarded with panoramic views of the surrounding mountains and valleys.

The route is in Roosevelt National Forest and, in contrast to Rocky Mountain National Park, dogs are permitted on

Rock outcropping along the way.

the trail. Both safety and courtesy suggest that leashes be employed.

GETTING THERE: From the junction of US 36 and Colorado 7, at the east side of Estes Park, proceed south roughly 7 miles on Colorado 7. The trailhead is on the west side of the highway—which is to the right when coming from Estes Park.

The trailhead is not well marked and the small indicator sign is not visible when coming from the north, until you are virtually even with it. There are four rock cuts, including a small one, after the mile 5 marker. The trailhead is just a few yards beyond the fourth rock cut.

Coming from the south, the trailhead is roughly 0.25 mile past the parking lots for Twin Sisters and Lily Lake. It is very close to the mile 6 marker and the trailhead sign is visible when coming from this direction.

There is limited parking at the trailhead, and it consists of unpaved areas along Colorado 7—just wide enough to allow

View from the summit of Lily Mountain.   PHOTO BY WARD LUTHI

parallel parking. If there is no convenient parking by the trailhead, you can look for spaces at the Twin Sisters or Lily Lake trailheads.

THE ROUTE: The trail initially runs to the north, with both ascending and descending sections. The lightly wooded terrain allows good views to the east and southeast. An apparent fork appears in the trail after a short distance. The lower trail is the correct route. (Long branches are laid across the upper route in the conventional way of indicating that an apparent path is not the trail.)

Eventually, there are a few switchbacks, followed by more ascending and descending sections, with a slight drift to the west. Interesting rock outcrops can be observed along this section as new views open up.

The trail comes to a large rock outcrop with a wide opening, which provides a nice view to the west and southwest. The viewpoint is a few yards off the trail, but there is nothing wrong with enjoying the scene and taking photos from this spot.

At this point, the trail turns 180 degrees to the south and starts up the spine of a ridge heading directly to the summit. The trail becomes a bit of a climb for the remaining distance.

Your hike ends with a rock scramble to the summit. A sign points to the rock climb. The optimal route up through the boulders is marked with small cairns.

Proceed very carefully as you go up, and descend the rock scramble with equal care. Return to the trailhead by following the same route in reverse.

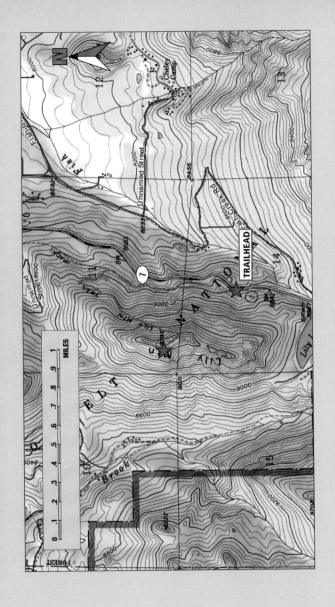

11. Lion Gulch Trail

BY JOHN GASCOYNE

MAPS	Trails Illustrated, Cache La Poudre/ Big Thompson, Number 101 USGS, Panorama Peak 7.5 minute
ELEVATION GAIN	1,200 feet (approx.)
RATING	Moderate
ROUND-TRIP DISTANCE	6.2 miles
ROUND-TRIP TIME	3.5 hours
NEAREST LANDMARK	US 36, mile marker 8

COMMENT: Lion Gulch Trail offers the best of two local worlds—the natural and the historic. You'll enjoy a beautiful 3-mile, largely uphill, trek through enchanting woods to the meadow area, where you'll visit with and pay homage to the spirits of incredibly hardy and dedicated homesteaders.

The first homestead that you're likely to encounter is the one settled by Sarah Walker. After burying her husband and children elsewhere, Sarah began a new life in these mountains—working the land in order to perfect her homesteader's claim upon it. She trekked several miles into the town of Lyons to sell butter and eggs, her only source of cash.

The signage at the trailhead is a bit vague—it spells the name of the trail as both Lyon Gulch and Lion Gulch. The former is an apparent tip of the hat to the town of Lyons, not that far away; the latter, and correct, name refers to the local mountain lions, whose tracks are often visible, especially in the soft sand along the meadow area. The Kingston Trio sang that ". . . the lion still rules the barranca (ravine)." Something similar can be said of Lion Gulch—where you won't see the lion, but she may have one sleepy eye on you, so don't let younger children out of your sight.

Meadows in the Homestead area.   PHOTO BY JOHN GASCOYNE

Close encounters of the backwoods kind are common—Lion Gulch Trail is very popular and draws enthusiasts from many urban areas. It is open to and used by bikers and equestrians as well as hikers. Horseback riders have the right of way over all other users. If the trail is narrow and you have to step aside for horse traffic, move to the uphill side and avoid swinging your trekking poles near the horses. Savvy riders will appreciate you talking quietly to them as a means of reassurance to their horses.

Hikers have the right of way over bikers, but I'm usually willing to concede this to the bikers, especially those who are bouncing downhill and struggling to maintain control. Dogs are allowed on the trail and are not required to be on leash. Leashes, however, make a good deal of sense—for the protection of your dog and for the comfort of other hikers, bikers, and riders.

There is an outhouse at the trailhead, but no other facilities.

GETTING THERE: From Estes Park, take US 36, on the south side of Lake Estes, and proceed in a generally southeastern direction to mile marker 8—a distance of about 8 miles beyond the lake. The trailhead will be on your right.

Relics from the homesteading era.

PHOTO BY JOHN GASCOYNE

From Loveland or Fort Collins, take Hwy 34 through Big Thompson Canyon to Mall Road, just before Lake Estes. Turn left and proceed to Hwy 36, less than a mile away. Turn left again and proceed to mile marker 8.

If you are coming from, Boulder, Longmont, or the Denver area, drive to Lyons and head northwesterly on US 36.

THE ROUTE: You'll enjoy an invigorating 3-mile hike through beautiful Colorado landscape, complete with three bridges and ten stream crossings. Although the initial part of your hike is downhill, you'll encounter lots of moderately serious uphill real estate. It would take both focus and determination to become lost on this trail—just stay on the obvious path until you reach the meadows, 3 miles away.

Soon after crossing the second bridge, the trail divides into a hiking portion and an equestrian portion. These two soon rejoin and remain a single trail for the rest of the way up to the meadows. To add a bit of variety to your hike, take one of these short diversions on the way up and the other on the way back down.

If you want to enjoy a longer hike and explore more, then the 3 miles to the meadow area can be the beginning, rather than the turnaround point, of your trek. From the meadows, you'll have multiple opportunities to hike a good deal more and explore the remains of the eight homesteads accessible from the trail.

To return, retrace your steps to the trailhead.

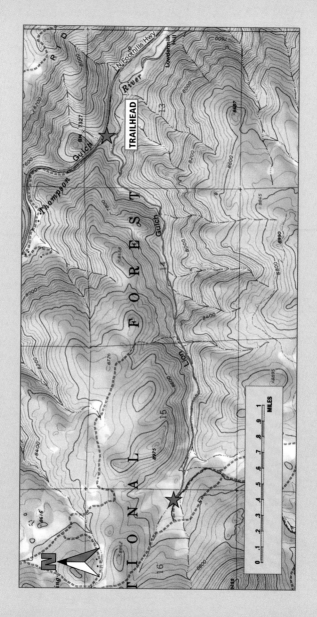

TRAILHEAD

12. Lookout Mountain Trail and Horsetooth Peak Trail

BY AMY CROW

MAPS	Trails Illustrated, Rocky Mountain National Park, Number 200 USGS, Allenspark Quadrangle 7.5 minute
ELEVATION GAIN	1,943 feet (approx.)
RATING	Moderate–difficult
ROUND-TRIP DISTANCE	6.8 miles
ROUND-TRIP TIME	4 hours
NEAREST LANDMARK	Meeker Lodge on Colorado 7

COMMENT: Lookout Mountain offers a secluded and little-traveled trail through a wooded area that leads to rocky outcroppings and fantastic views. The path has areas where elevation gain can be strenuous, but it is tempered by stretches that skirt the mountain.

About halfway up, Mount Meeker starts to make an appearance to the west and Twin Sisters Peaks are visible to the east. The summit of the aptly named Lookout Mountain offers 360-degree views of these peaks, a full view of Wild Basin to the south, and views of the many peaks that fringe this amazing valley. These peaks include St. Vrain Mountain, Mount Audubon, Copeland Mountain, Isolation Peak, and Mount Alice. To the west, Mount Meeker, at 13,911 feet, is an imposing presence.

Coming down from the summit of Lookout Mountain, about 0.5 mile down trail, you will see a tree with the initials "HT" carved in it and two cairns; these lead the way to Horsetooth Peak. The path to the summit of Horsetooth Peak is an easy jaunt. The rock formations on Lookout

Lookout Mountain summit with Mount Meeker in background.

PHOTO BY AMY CROW

Mountain and Horsetooth Peak offer plenty of "chair-like" areas for eating your lunch and enjoying the view.

GETTING THERE: At the junction of US 34 and US 36 on the east side of Estes Park, turn south onto Colorado 7. Stay on this highway for 11.8 miles to Meeker Park. Turn on 113N directly across from Meeker Lodge. Travel on this dirt road for 0.6 mile to the trailhead.

THE ROUTE: The trailhead starts on private land but soon enters Rocky Mountain National Park. The trail splits, with the left fork heading to Wild Basin and the right spur leading to the Lookout Mountain Trail. The way is well marked by signage.

The trail stays in deep woods, gaining altitude. Uphill parts of the trail alternate with stretches of flat trail that skirt the

Lush vegetation along the way.

PHOTO BY AMY CROW

mountain. Several small streams cross the path, creating patches of intense green moss, mushrooms, and an array of ever-changing wildflowers.

As you gain altitude, amazing views come into play. The statuesque Mount Meeker is visible to the west. To the east, the Twin Sisters Peaks dominate the landscape and the eastern plains can be seen beyond.

Around the 2.7-mile mark, look for a gouge in a tree in which the initials "HT" are faintly carved. Cairns on either side of the trail seem out of place at this point, but they mark the trail to Horsetooth Peak. Veer to the left and follow a tranquil and shady 0.25-mile trail directly to its summit.

Once back on the main trail, climb up Squally Ridge—a sandy and windblown saddle. The picturesque trees in this area are crooked and misshapen, a product of untold years of wind exposure. For the hiker, however, this flat and sunny area is welcome. Stay to the left and follow the cairns to the summit of Lookout Mountain. The first rock outcropping provides good photo ops of Mount Meeker. Continue to your right, carefully climbing rock slabs in order to view Wild Basin and points beyond. Once there, enjoy some sit-down time on nature-made chairs.

Retrace your steps to return to the trailhead.

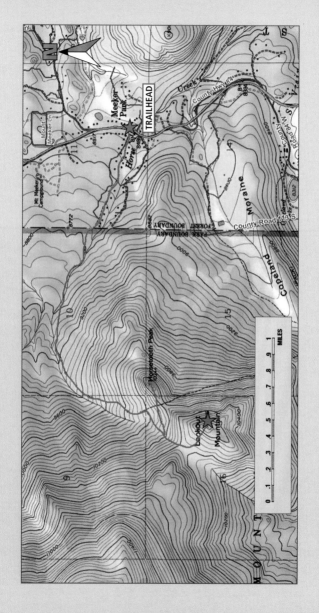

13. Meadow Mountain Trail
14. St. Vrain Mountain Trail

BY KURT WORRELL

Editor's Note: Due to their proximity to one another, these two trails are being considered together. We are using the saddle between the two mountains as the most convenient reference point for your hiking.

MAPS	Trails Illustrated, Rocky Mountain National Park, Number 200 USGS, Allenspark Quadrangle 7.5 Minute
ELEVATION GAIN	Saddle only—2,400 feet—(13.4 percent average grade)
ROUND-TRIP DISTANCE	Saddle only—6.1 miles
ROUND-TRIP TIME	Saddle only—4.5 hours
ELEVATION GAIN	Saddle to St. Vrain Mountain— 925 feet
ROUND-TRIP DISTANCE	Saddle to St. Vrain Mountain— 2.28 miles
ROUND-TRIP TIME	Saddle to St. Vrain Mountain— 2 hours (23 percent grade from the trail to the peak)
ELEVATION GAIN	Saddle to Meadow Mountain— 400 feet
ROUND-TRIP DISTANCE	Saddle to Meadow Mountain— 0.52 miles
ROUND-TRIP TIME	Saddle to Meadow Mountain— 1 hour (25 percent grade from the trail to the peak)
RATING	Moderate to the saddle; difficult if combined with either or both peaks
NEAREST LANDMARK	Allenspark

Near the top of Meadow Mountain.
PHOTO BY WARD LUTHI

COMMENT: The Allenspark area is situated south of Rocky Mountain National Park (RMNP) and north of the Indian Peaks Wilderness Area (IPWA) along Colorado 7. Being away from these high traffic areas provides access to the same terrain and scenery without any of the crowds.

Along Colorado 7, there are a variety of US Forest Service (USFS) campgrounds available for use throughout the year, which makes early access to the backcountry convenient. To the east of Allenspark, access is available to the Taylor Mountain area and to the deep canyons of the combined Roaring Fork River, Horse Creek, North St. Vrain Creek, and Rock Creek basins.

Situated between the North and Middle St. Vrain River basins, the St. Vrain Mountain Trail provides access to high elevation views of many of the peaks in RMNP, including Longs Peak and Mount Meeker, as well as direct access to the northern portion of the IPWA. The trail also affords panoramic views of the lakes, glaciers, and peaks of the Wild Basin area.

Because of the abundant water in the area, the foliage is mixed aspen grove and ponderosa pine forest with varieties of riparian foliage. In the spring, the forested areas and deep canyons provide a safe haven for the heavy winter snow that accumulates here. During summer, the heavily forested terrain provides significant relief from the hot summer sun, and in the fall the colors here match those of any high alpine area in the Front Range.

The views from the saddle between Meadow Mountain and St. Vrain Mountain are spectacular, making this portion of the trip alone well worth the effort. Adding the ascent to St. Vrain Mountain provides another vantage point for Wild Basin, a new view to the south into IPWA, and an unobstructed view of the Longs Peak region.

The hike to Meadow Mountain provides an even better view of the south side of Mount Meeker and Longs Peak, as well as an improved view of the peaks north of Mount Copeland. Any collection of these destinations will provide memories and photographs that you can benchmark against the best destinations in the United States.

GETTING THERE: From the junction of US 34 and US 36 on the east side of downtown Estes Park, drive east on US 36 for 0.3 mile and take a right on Colorado 7. Travel south on Colorado 7 for 14.6 miles, arriving at the Allenspark turnoff on the right side of the road. (Along the way you will pass the Lily Lake, Twin Sisters, Longs Peak, and Wild Basin trailheads.) When you arrive at Allenspark, turn right into Allenspark and follow the paved road as it sweeps left, parallel to Colorado 7. The first roadway to the right will be labeled Ski Road/CR 107. Turn right onto Ski Road and follow this single lane dirt road as it winds through the houses of Allenspark. After 0.5 mile, the road will straighten as you leave the town. There it junctions with a much wider dirt road that can be taken sharply left (CR 107-E) or straight (CR 107). Continue straight onto CR 107 for 1.2 miles to a Y in the road, marked by a sign for CR 116. Take the right fork and continue 0.5 mile up the gently winding road until you arrive at the well-marked St. Vrain Mountain trailhead

St. Vrain Mountain from the saddle.

parking area. Parking is limited to about 10 cars and there are no facilities. All of the dirt roads mentioned here are passable by 2WD vehicles.

THE ROUTE: The St. Vrain Mountain Trail is well marked with USFS signs and is accessible from the west side of the parking area. The first 2.25 miles of the trail consist mostly of heavily wooded pine forests with aspen groves wherever there is water available. The well-traveled trail is situated on the south facing slope, but the trees provide adequate cover from the hot summer sun. The trail climbs steadily from the trailhead to the saddle between Meadow Mountain and St. Vrain Mountain, with a 14 percent average grade. Creek water is available along the trail between the 1.0- and 2.4-mile points as the trail crosses the low point of the drainage being climbed. The trail crosses the creek several times on stone paths; you may need waterproof boots depending on the trip date. (Note—any creek or lake water in Colorado should be filtered before being consumed.)

At 0.65 mile from the trailhead, two signs indicate that you are entering IPWA, and as such you must adhere to the IPWA rules and regulations. At 1.0 mile, switchbacks begin

Indian Peaks Wilderness Area peaks: Audubon, Paiute, and Sawtooth mountains as seen from St. Vrain Mountain. PHOTO BY KURT WORRELL

the climb from the base of the valley to the saddle. A long switchback to the south returns to the north at about 2.4 miles. At this point, the trail turns directly west and climbs the last trail segment to the saddle. Meadow Mountain is the 11,632-foot-high point directly north from the saddle, while St. Vrain Mountain is the higher peak seen to the right of the trail that heads south from the saddle. It is suggested that St. Vrain Mountain be climbed first so that Meadow Mountain can either be climbed or bypassed on the descent.

Once you have reached the saddle, as you travel southward along the trail a sign will indicate your entrance into RMNP. Further along the gradual climb from the saddle toward the left shoulder of St. Vrain Mountain you will encounter a set of signs indicating that you are leaving RMNP and re-entering IPWA. Shortly thereafter you will pass through a small group of subalpine firs and junipers. Upon exiting the pines to the south, you should immediately look to ascend onto the east ridge of St. Vrain Mountain. There is no maintained trail to the summit so you should make your own way, keeping your direction of travel roughly in line with the RMNP boundary markers that rise along the eastern ridge.

On the trail from Meadow Mountain to St. Vrain Mountain.

Once at the top, a stone shelter provides a break from the predominant easterly blowing wind. The panoramic views from this point are spectacular and range from Beaver Reservoir (southeast) to Mount Audubon (south) to Sawtooth, Elk Tooth, and Mount Copeland (west), and on to Chiefs Head Peak, Longs Peak, Mount Meeker, and Twin Sisters to the north and east. Finch and Sandbeach Lakes are clearly visible when looking north into the Wild Basin area.

On the descent from the St. Vrain summit, it is recommended that you again follow along the RMNP boundary markers for the bulk of the descent, moving southward to avoid the junipers near the trail. At all points on the descent, the trail below is clearly visible. Return to the saddle along the same route used during the ascent. Once back at the saddle, if you choose to ascend Meadow Mountain, continue down until the trail starts a descent back to the starting trailhead. At this point, proceed across the

St. Vrain Mountain.

tundra northward (left) to the base of the mountain. The western half of the mountain is devoid of junipers. There is no maintained route to the top, and it is suggested that you make your way up keeping your line of travel on the south flank of the mountain within the scattered junipers. The slope consists of grass and small boulders for the first two-thirds of the ascent. Higher up the peak the terrain consists of medium and large boulders.

The top of Meadow Mountain is similar to St. Vrain Mountain. There is a stone shelter for protection from the wind, as well as weather measurement equipment. The peak provides an unobstructed view of Twin Sisters, Mount Meeker, Longs Peak, and the peaks to the west. It also provides an unobstructed view of the peaks north of Mount Copeland, which were not visible from the top of St. Vrain Mountain. Descend by retracing your steps back to the saddle.

From the saddle, descend and return to the trailhead following the same trail used during the ascent.

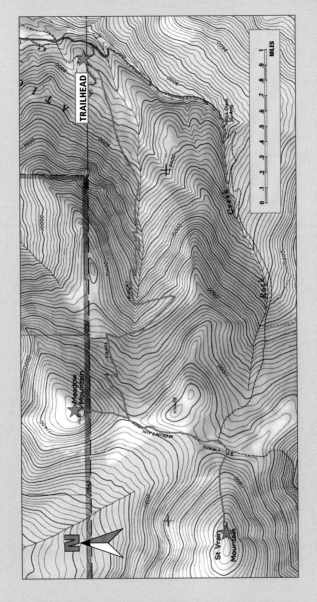

15. Round Mountain Trail

BY RUDY SCHMIEDT

MAPS	Trails Illustrated, Cache La Poudre/ Big Thompson, Number 101 USGS, Drake Quadrangle 7.5 Minute
ELEVATION GAIN	2,700 feet
RATING	Moderate–difficult
ROUND-TRIP DISTANCE	9.5 miles
ROUND-TRIP TIME	5–6 hours
NEAREST LANDMARK	Loveland

COMMENT: If you want an intense workout up a huge summit in the Colorado foothills, this hike is for you. This trek is snow-free most of the year, although it gets icy in the spring-time. The trail is unrelentingly steep most of the way, climbing through forests of ponderosa pine, Douglas fir, and some aspen. You will encounter spectacular granite formations just past the halfway point. Several interpretive signs are found along the way. You may see blue grouse, deer, black bears, rattlesnakes, and maybe even an elusive mountain lion. Round Mountain is frequently listed as "Sheep Mountain" or even as "Dome Mountain" on some maps.

GETTING THERE: From Loveland, drive 12 miles west on US 34 to Viestenz-Smith Mountain Park, at mile 79.5. Then travel 0.1 mile farther west and turn left (south) on the well-marked dirt road to the parking lot. From Estes Park, take US 34 east, about 24 miles or so—depending on your starting point —and look for the dirt road just before mile 79.5.

THE ROUTE: Walk up on the dirt road about 0.2 mile and go south (left) on the summit trail. Ascend steeply through a

Rock cut on the Round Mountain Trail.

ponderosa pine and Douglas fir forest, climbing above the Big Thompson River. At the 1.0-mile marker, there are good views of the canyon and Palisade Mountain (8,264 feet).

At 2.5 miles up the trail, great views to the east open up. Here the trail cuts through a gap in a massive granitic outcropping. The trail descends slightly and, at the 3.0-mile marker, a perennial spring is located. It is always a good water source, except in the most severe drought. (Editor's note: it is suggested that water from any natural source in Colorado be run through a filtering system.) Some mining activity took place around the Three Mile Spring area about 1900, but very little evidence of this exists now.

A low pass is surmounted at 3.5 miles. The trail climbs the southeast side of the mountain, going past interesting granitic intrusions into the older schist, which predominates here. These rocks are around 1.75 billion years old.

There are some views of Pinewood Reservoir and Stone Mountain. On a clear day, Pikes Peak can be seen 110 miles to the south. The main Round Mountain Trail continues climbing steeply to the tall summit cairn at 4.75 miles and the 8,450-foot summit.

Snow-covered Round Mountain summit marker.   PHOTO BY RUDY SCHMIEDT

The true summit has no real views, but just 100 feet west and slightly downhill from the top there are good views of Longs Peak, the Continental Divide, Hallet Peak, Flattop Mountain, and even the Mummy Range.

For a view of the Big Thompson Canyon, bushwhack 0.1 mile to the north from the summit. The river is 2,700 feet below. This climb is a great workout up a fascinating foothill. It's always an adventure.

If you have extra time, or just wish to do a shorter trip, consider climbing Stone Mountain. This off-trail route leaves the Round Mountain Trail at about 3.5 miles from the trailhead. Here a low pass is encountered, with the Round Mountain Trail turning sharply west (to the right). An off-trail route for the adventurous leads 0.75 mile east-southeast up and over "Middle Mountain" (7,709 feet) to the summit of spectacular Stone Mountain (7,655 feet). This sharp, rocky peak has great views but requires a bit of Class 3 rock scrambling near the summit. Stone Mountain is a great destination in itself.

Return to the trailhead by retracing your steps.

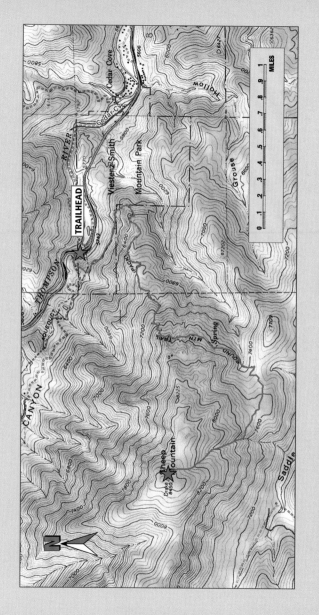

16. Sandbeach Lake

BY ALAN APT*

MAPS	Trails Illustrated, Rocky Mountain National Park, Number 200 USGS, Allenspark Quadrangle 7.5 minute
ELEVATION GAIN	1,945 feet (starting from 8,300 feet)
RATING	Moderate
ROUND-TRIP DISTANCE	8.4 miles
ROUND-TRIP TIME	5–6 hours
NEAREST LANDMARK	Wild Basin Entry Station, Rocky Mountain National Park

COMMENT: Can it be true—a spectacular mountain setting framed by towering (13,911-foot) Mount Meeker and a sandy beach as well? Yes, it is true, but there are caveats: the beach is composed of high altitude grit from nearby hills and the crystalline water, while inviting, is quite chilly.

To reach Sandbeach Lake, you'll enjoy a scenic hike with views of Wild Basin and Copeland Mountain, punctuated by beautiful rock outcroppings and the intermittent music of cascading streams. Close-in backcountry campsites make this route a favorite for short backpacking adventures.

GETTING THERE: From Estes Park or Loveland: go to Colorado 7 (off of US 36 at the west end of Lake Estes); follow Colorado 7 south 12 miles to the Wild Basin entrance of RMNP—located on the west side of the highway. From Lyons, take Colorado 7 generally west and then northwest for approximately 25 miles to Allenspark. Proceed past Allenspark a short 2 miles to the Wild Basin entrance.

The beach in the mountains.

PHOTO BY ALAN APT

After passing through the fee-required entrance station, take an immediate right into the parking area for the trailhead—located on the north edge of the lot. Restroom facilities are available here.

THE ROUTE: The trail climbs steeply at the outset, gaining 200 feet in 0.25 mile, at which point it turns to the west. This section provides nice views of Copeland Mountain, some beaver ponds, Willow Creek canyon, and the slopes of Meadow Mountain to the south. The trail then traverses west while gradually climbing through an area sparsely populated with ponderosa pine and affording a brief view of colorful Wild Basin and distant ridgelines.

Over the next 1.4 miles you'll climb a total of 700 feet through more dense stands of conifer and aspen trees. The

On the trail to Sand Beach.   PHOTO BY ALAN APT

trail then levels off, at around 9,000 feet, at the intersection of the Meeker Park Trail.

After the intersection, the trail becomes steeper and heads in a more northwesterly direction. This section is enhanced by interesting rock outcroppings and quaking aspen.

Your next landmarks are the Hole in the Wall backcountry campsites and Campers Creek. Enjoy the riparian music of the cascading stream as the trail climbs slowly to 9,600 feet and the Campers Creek and Beaver Mill campsites. A footbridge will carry you across the creek; then the trail climbs slowly—and then steeply—into the Hunter Creek drainage, to almost 10,000 feet, and the named campsites. There is no fishing allowed in Hunter Creek, but Sandbeach Lake is a catch and release fishin' hole.

After crossing Hunter Creek on another footbridge, the trail continues to steeply climb the last 350 feet to the gleaming lake—at about 10,300 feet and nestled in below the stunning mountain backdrop. There is a trail around the lake, leading to more campsites.

To return to the trailhead, simply retrace your steps.

---

*Editor's note: Alan Apt is the author of the Colorado Mountain Club Press book, *Snowshoe Routes: Colorado's Front Range, Second Edition*

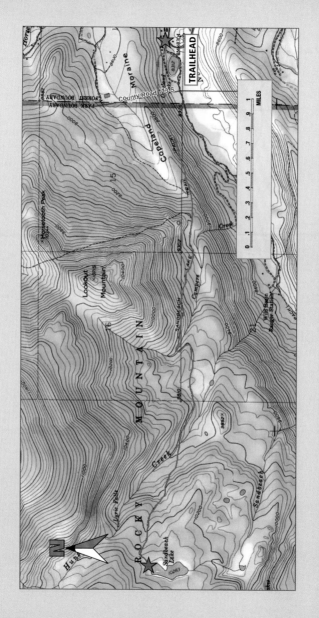

17. Signal Mountain Trail

BY DANIELLE POOLE

MAPS	Trails Illustrated, Poudre River/ Cameron Pass, Number 112 USGS, Pingree Park Quadrangle 7.5 minute (See also USGS Crystal Mountain and Glen Haven maps)
ELEVATION GAIN	3,869 feet
RATING	Difficult (strenuous)
ROUND-TRIP DISTANCE	13.4 miles
ROUND-TRIP TIME	9 hours
NEAREST LANDMARK	Glen Haven/Trails End Ranch Boys Camp

COMMENT: The Signal peaks were named during the late 1800s when pioneers thought they saw smoke signals originating from their summits. For most hikers, this is a very challenging trail: first, because of the length—it's a 6.7-mile destination—and second, the 3,869-foot elevation gain.

Keeping these two points in mind, the summits of North and South Signal mountains are well worth your time and effort. The easy sections might give the impression that it's a walk in the park. The rest, however, is high-stepping, uphill walking over rock-strewn trails that bring dry riverbeds to mind. Once you're past the Bulwark Ridge section, however, you can start to breathe a bit more easily and celebrate the last section to the summit. Signal Mountain Trail destinations are two close-proximity peaks, separated by a 0.5-mile saddle.

The benefit of hiking to both peaks is the 360-degree view offered from each summit, even though their access is monumental—as in extremely challenging—to the average hiker, who will travel from 7,430 feet up to 11,299 feet.

Lower section of Signal Mountain Trail.   PHOTO BY DANIELLE POOLE

GETTING THERE: From the intersections of US 34 and US 36 on the eastern end of Estes Park, travel north on Wonderview Avenue (US 34) to MacGregor Avenue/Devils Gulch Road and turn right onto Devils Gulch Road (County Road 43). Drive 8.2 miles to the village of Glen Haven. Continue 2.5 miles farther and turn left at Dunraven Glade Road. Consider the neighbors and travel slowly on this dirt road 2 miles to the trailhead, located at the cul-de-sac parking lot.

THE ROUTE: At the end of the parking lot, pass through a narrow span at the gate and walk 0.25 mile up the dirt road, where you'll see the trail sign to Bulwark Ridge Trail. Begin your ascent through the sage-fragrant, dry landscape, dotted with fire-scarred trees and, depending on the season, laced with colorful wildflowers. A quarter mile into the hike, turn around and see Glen Haven's panoramic westerly view and the Estes Park area in the distant west—including the prominent Twin Sisters, Mount Meeker, and Longs Peak.

As you get into the wooded areas of the hike, these sights become only fond memories. After 1.0 mile, you'll arrive at a junction of the Miller Fork and Indian trails. Stay left on

View from the north summit to the south summit.   PHOTO BY DANIELLE POOLE

the Bulwark Ridge Trail (#928). Ahead lies mile after mile of aspen and pine, intermingled with an earthy meadow now and then, but mostly wooded areas that are either thick and shaded or steep and sunny. Upon leaving the thick, shaded woods, you'll face the rocky ascent, where parts may be blocked by fallen trees. If so, go around the windblown trees to find the trail.

Your first view of South Signal Mountain is nearby, at the 4.5-mile point. This sighting will beckon you on and, even with the knowledge that you still have quite an elevation gain ahead, you'll believe the hardships you endured the previous five hours were not in vain.

The temporarily descending trail turns right (north) and leads below the south summit toward North Signal Mountain. The trail becomes easy as it passes through wind-twisted trees and onto the tundra. As you follow the gentle ascent toward the north summit, you'll gratefully arrive at the farthest point northeast. Turn left here to find the highest elevation marker behind you, at the western edge of North Signal Mountain, where there's a three-foot-high, stacked-rock windbreak. From there, enjoy a 360-degree view that includes Lookout Mountain, directly north, and a great many other glorious parks and peaks.

Enjoy lunch at this vantage point before heading back. As an alternative, you can backtrack to South Signal Mountain to get your fill of the extraordinary view you've earned as a reward for your valiant efforts.

Return to the trailhead by retracing your steps. The descent will take only half the time the ascent did.

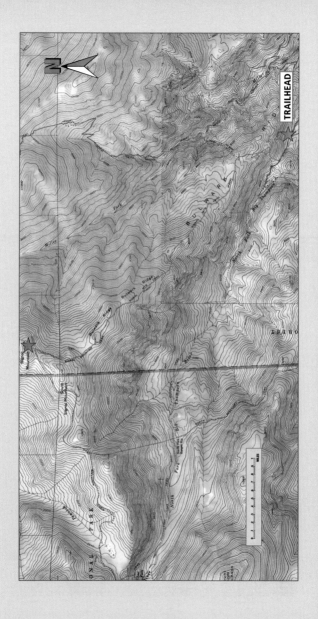

18. Twin Owls Loop

BY DANIELLE POOLE

MAPS	Trails Illustrated, Rocky Mountain National Park, Number 200 USGS, Estes Park Quadrangle 7.5 minute
ELEVATION GAIN	2,829 feet
RATING	Moderate–difficult
ROUND-TRIP DISTANCE	11.9 miles
ROUND-TRIP TIME	7.9 hours
NEAREST LANDMARK	MacGregor Ranch

COMMENT: The Twin Owls Loop offers a variety of terrain and ecosystems, from elevations of 7,696 to 9,100 feet. Start at the Lumpy Ridge trailhead and circle either clockwise or counterclockwise. Both directions have challenging elevations but, considering the length of the trip, it is recommended that you travel counterclockwise in order to begin with the steepest ascent.

GETTING THERE: From the intersection of US 34 and US 36 on the east side of Estes Park, take Wonderview Avenue (US 34) north and turn right onto MacGregor Avenue. Drive 1.3 miles to the Lumpy Ridge trailhead on the left.

THE ROUTE: Hiking to Gem Lake first provides you with a fantastic view of the entire Estes Park valley. Lumpy Ridge is a series of eroded rocks about 4.0 miles long by 1.0 mile wide, replete with amazing shapes.

An hour into the ascent you'll see a 10-foot-high rock with a hole in it—referred to as Paul Bunyan's Boot—and, at 1.7 miles you'll arrive at Gem Lake—a natural amphitheater enhanced by a picturesque pond.

The Needles under a storm cloud.

Continuing past Gem Lake, you'll start a descent to the east. Here the trail turns away from Lumpy Ridge, but returns to the north and then heads west. The descent takes you through lower elevations and you can see across to the north—past the drainage you'll be crossing—to distant ridges. On the flats, 0.2 mile after Gem Lake, you'll see a sign to Balanced Rock. This is a 0.75-mile optional spur that ends at a precarious rock outcropping. Retrace your steps to return to the Twin Owls Loop.

After a while, the trail descends into a shady wetlands area. Cross a log bridge over a refreshing creek and linger to take photos and enjoy the mossy rocks that line the creek. After you climb the trail out of the creek area, you'll come to an aspen-skirted wildflower meadow. The trail will pass a couple of camping spots. The one that's closest to the north side is Rabbit Ears, named for a rock formation to the south (left).

When you come to a second log bridge, with a sign in front of it marked "Horse Crossing," you'll enjoy one of the nicest views of the entire loop—and an excellent place to have lunch.

To your right now is a looming rock formation that acts as a buttress to the north ridge. Nearby is Bridal Veil Falls

Panorama of Gem Lake.   PHOTO BY DANIELLE POOLE

Trail. At this junction, the Twin Owls Loop Trail narrows—take the left fork and leave the valley to begin your ascent through a shady forest with much drier ground.

Enjoy the earthy smells and scents of ponderosa pine during your switchback journey. After a mile or so, you'll see sky through the trees and you'll come to a ridge. The clearing ahead is the saddle that leads to the next junction. Take the left fork and meet the eastern leg of the loop. You'll be in the trees for 2.8 miles, but will begin to see geological wonders named for their familiar shapes: The Pear, The Book, and, closer to the end, the trail's namesake—The Twin Owls.

Just before you get out of the trees, you'll come to a gate that marks the boundary of private property—the MacGregor Ranch. As you slow your pace to gaze up at Lumpy Ridge, you'll come to the eastern edge of the fenced meadow. You'll pass a paved parking lot historically used as a trailhead, but now privately used by the National Forest Service workers who reside nearby. To the right of the driveway you'll see your next trail marker, indicating a narrow path through aspen trees. Considering that your destination is the Lumpy Ridge trailhead, turn right to end up back at your parking place.

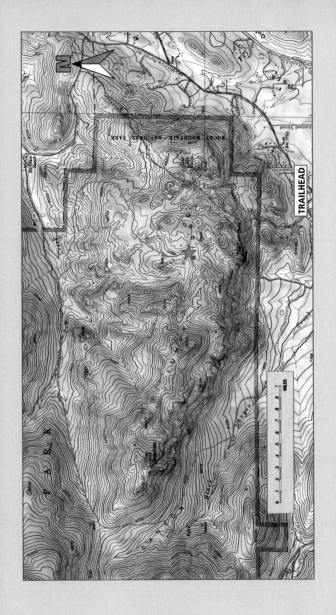

TRAILHEAD

ROCKY MOUNTAIN NATIONAL PARK

PARK

MILES
0 1 2 3 4 5 6 7 8 9

N

19. Twin Sisters Trail

BY JACK POWERS

MAPS	Trails Illustrated, Rocky Mountain National Park, Number 200 USGS, Longs Peak Quadrangle 7.5 Minute
ELEVATION GAIN	2,338 feet
RATING	Moderate
ROUND-TRIP DISTANCE	7.4 miles
ROUND-TRIP TIME	4.5 hours
NEAREST LANDMARK	Estes Park

COMMENT: Twin Sisters Peaks are located on the eastern edge of Rocky Mountain National Park. It is the only peak in the park on the east side of Colorado 7. It can be seen from many different perspectives within the park, such as the overlook at Rainbow Curve on Trail Ridge Road, and from cities on the plains 30 or more miles away.

The trail takes the hiker through an ever-changing forest and finally above the timberline itself. As the trail climbs, the forest shifts from lodgepole pines to spruces and firs, and then limber pines at even higher elevations.

Despite the harsh climate at this high elevation, plants and animals survive among the rocks and tundra. Flowers bloom in rock crevices and on the tundra. If you are lucky, you may observe grazing Rocky Mountain bighorn sheep. Chirping pikas can be seen scurrying through the rocks, collecting food for the coming winter.

Marmots and ground squirrels live at the very peak of Twin Sisters. They are interested in your snacks, but you do them no favor by feeding them. Watch your backpacks, because these critters can be guilty of breaking and entering should they get a whiff of food.

A view of the Mummy Range from the Twin Sisters summit.

The views along the trail are a photographer's joy. Longs Peak and the Estes Cone are visible throughout the hike. The Mummy Range and other more distant peaks become visible at higher elevations. Estes Park, Lake Estes, and the YMCA of the Rockies appear in miniature below.

GETTING THERE: From the east side of Estes Park and the junction of US 34 and US 36, go southeasterly to the junction of US 36 and Colorado 7. Drive roughly 6.3 miles south on Colorado 7. The Twin Sisters trailhead will be on the left (east) side of the road and nearly opposite the parking lot for Lily Lake. Follow the road up the hill and park on the right side of the road. Do not park in the circle at the end of the road as it is used for a turn-around area.

If you are coming from the south, the trailhead is roughly 13 miles from the junction of Colorado 7 and Colorado 72 and will be on the right (east) side of the road.

THE ROUTE: To reach the start of the trail, walk up the road and turn left (upward) at the turn-around circle. A kiosk

A high meadow on Twin Sisters.   PHOTO BY JACK POWERS

marks the start of the trail. The trail starts in a forest of lodgepole pines, which provide nice shade on a hot day. After three switchbacks, there is a long, fairly straight segment, which has an excellent viewpoint (and photo op) of Longs Peak and Estes Cone.

The nature of the forest changes as the trail relentlessly climbs. Toward the top of the forested section there are small meadows with good views of the valleys below and the mountains to the west and northwest.

There are well over 20 switchbacks before the trail emerges from the trees and enters a boulder field. Careful attention must be paid to footing along this area. It is best to stop walking if you want to take in the views above the timberline.

The trail eventually reaches a saddle between two peaks. There is a route to the top of the western peak, which can be picked up behind the stone building. The small area on top is a good spot for snacking and photography. Keep a sharp eye on the weather and start to descend at the first sign of an incoming storm. Return to the trailhead by retracing your steps.

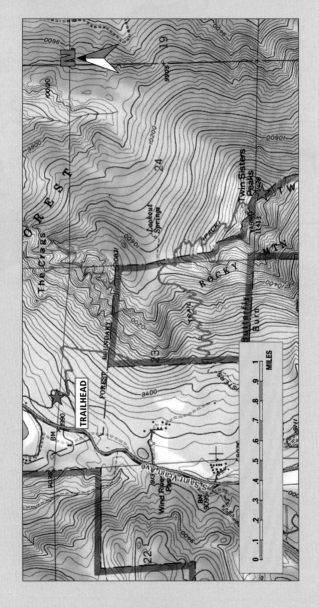

20. West Creek Falls Trail

BY RENEE QUEBBEMAN

MAPS	Trails Illustrated, Rocky Mountain National Park, Number 200 USGS, Estes Park Quadrangle 7.5 Minute
ELEVATION GAIN	1,090 feet gained (800 feet lost one way)
RATING	Easy–moderate
ROUND-TRIP DISTANCE	4.4 miles
ROUND-TRIP TIME	3 hours (by the legs of a slow hiker with a 2-year-old)
NEAREST LANDMARK	McGraw Ranch

COMMENT: West Creek Falls Trail begins at the McGraw Research Center, formerly the McGraw Ranch, and, later a dude ranch circa 1920. The National Park Service purchased the ranch in 1988 to renovate it for scientists whose research helps preserve the natural resources of Rocky Mountain National Park. Though years have passed, you can still imagine the lively goings on as you walk past the historically preserved rustic cabins and into the rugged landscape. This trailhead also provides access to Bridal Veil Falls, Gem Lake, and Lawn Lake.

GETTING THERE: From points on the Front Range (Longmont, Loveland, Fort Collins, and more) head towards Estes Park using US 34, through Loveland, and up the lower part of Big Thompson Canyon. Approximately 17 miles from Loveland, at the town of Drake, take County Road 43 toward Glen Haven. This route avoids Estes Park traffic and affords a scenic journey with views of log homes, horse farms, and quaint Glen Haven—where you can still enjoy a 25-cent cup of coffee. This route also provides access to the

A cool but refreshing dip.

PHOTO BY JON QUEBBEMAN

backside of Crosier Mountain, with three trailheads on the left. County Road 43 is a narrow, winding road with few shoulders, so please be mindful of bikers. Follow County Road 43 for 11.5 miles after Drake to a right-hand turn onto McGraw Ranch Road. After 2.2 miles of gravel (includes washboard) you'll see roadside parking, limited to approximately 15 spaces. Amenities include an emergency phone and a pit privy about 100 yards west on Cow Creek Trail.

THE ROUTE: West Creek Falls is an out-and-back hike and offers great diversity. The trail starts beyond the McGraw Ranch Cabins, along Cow Creek Trail. Near the last cabin, the West Creek Falls Trail heads north along the North Boundary Trail. It begins with a steady climb for about 0.7 mile, to a saddle through an open, spruce-laden landscape.

The trail is sandy and narrow, with loose stones—not a great option for trail running. Although not excessively traveled, it's well maintained and signed. A few hundred yards past the saddle you'll enter the Comanche Peak Wilderness Area. Along the first climb, look back and see the Longs Peak ridgeline. Past the saddle summit there is a steep downhill. Nature seems to change immediately as you descend: there is a fairy-like quality to the trail, decorated with copious shade plants, trees, moss, and mushrooms. Loose stone continues here; mind your footing and use poles.

Crossing a rustic bridge.

PHOTO BY JON QUEBBEMAN

Views are spectacular, with Mount Dickinson visible towards the northwest. The end of this downhill finds you at the stream crossing of West Creek, mile 1.3. Then the trail heads west. West Creek becomes your trail-mate on your left. Travel along the creek to a fork, at mile 1.6, where the North Boundary Trail continues to the right (north) and the West Creek Falls Trail begins on the left (west). Here you'll find a boulder-covered, colorful slope—a lush *Sound of Music* section. This is the last leg before you reach the falls. You will see signs as you re-enter RMNP.

The falls include two sets of small falls and pools. The upper fall is the end, at 2.2 miles. You can reach the top of the 20-foot-high rock face by skirting up the right-hand side—a great place for a rest and lunch. The pools appear made to host bathing beauties . . . but only if you are a penguin! I'm from Maine, and I think it's cold. So you may make it in for a quick dip, but it is by no means a swimming hole. This is a beautiful destination, and my opinion is that children 8 and older would find it's a fun adventure. There are plenty of places for kids to climb and get dirty in relative safety. However, the hike itself and the falls will be a bit difficult for younger hikers; supervised children older than 3 or 4 should be fine. I did find myself having to back pack my little girl the entire time. A romantic family hike indeed.

To return, retrace your steps to the trailhead. This is one of the rare day hikes that includes a significant uphill on the return, so save some energy for the finish.

About the Author

Ward Luthi grew up in Rantoul, Illinois, deep in the heart of some of the finest farmland in the world. Known for its deep, rich soil, the land in east central Illinois was also, for the most part, well, flat. The nearest town, which Ward could easily see, was aptly named Flatville. Still, there were tracts of forest and small creeks to explore and Ward did his best to wander these areas as often as possible.

At the advanced age of 10, Ward and his family drove west to explore the wonders of Rocky Mountain National Park. Ward's first view of the Rockies, massively perched on the horizon, generated a spark of passion for the outdoors—a spark that became a lifetime fire. Those two weeks exploring the lakes, peaks, and forests in RMNP

A pika on the rocks.   PHOTO BY MARLENE BORNEMAN

Kings of the mountain.   PHOTO BY MARLENE BORNEMAN

captured Ward's soul and eventually led him to move to Colorado and a career in adventure travel and environmental advocacy.

Ward has trained with the National Outdoor Leadership School (NOLS), headquartered out of Lander, Wyoming, worked as an instructor and course director for Hurricane Island Outward Bound, and served as a staff member for the President's Commission on Americans Outdoors in Washington, DC. In addition to trail books, Ward has authored books on fitness and walking and adventure travel and appeared in exercise videos with Leslie Sansone.

Ward currently operates Walking The World, which he founded in 1987, a company dedicated to guiding adventurous souls over 50 on small group adventures around the world. As a way to give back, he founded 1Stove.org, a nonprofit dedicated to planting trees, building schools, and providing clean-burning cook stoves to families in Central America.

In his spare time, Ward can be found on the trails in RMNP or in his home away from home—the canyons of southeast Utah.

"Don't think I need a permit."

PHOTO BY JON QUEBBEMAN

Checklist

THE BEST ESTES PARK HIKES

On the Lion Gulch Trail.   PHOTO BY JOHN GASCOYNE

Marmot posing for the camera.